SOLZHENITSYN: POLITICS AND FORM

SOLZHENITSYN,

POLITICS AND FORM

FRANCIS BARKER

First published 1977 by
THE MACMILLAN PRESS LTD
London and Basingstoke
Associated companies in Delhi
Dublin Hong Kong Johannesburg Lagos
Melbourne New York Singapore Tokyo

Photoset, printed and bound
in Great Britain by
REDWOOD BURN LIMITED
Trowbridge & Esher

British Library Cataloguing in Publication Data

Barker, Francis
  Solzhenitsyn
  1. Solzhenitsyn, Aleksandr Isaevich—Criticism
  and interpretation
  891.7'3'44   PG3488.04Z/

  ISBN 0–333–21242–8

Contents

Preface

The work of any contemporary Soviet writer must be defined by its relationship to Stalinism. For the critic, and for the writer, this is not a personal choice but an historical task. It is a founding assumption of this study that it is impossible to make intelligible any work of literature unless its radical sociality is acknowledged and investigated. But there are various ways in which this definition may be approached, and I have adopted a particular, somewhat limited, way of treating the literature-society nexus. In his Introduction to Henri Arvon's book *Marxist Esthetics* the American critic Fredric Jameson enumerates four projects that a Marxist literary criticism should undertake; two of them are relevant here. In the critical study of literary works of the past 'we attempt to determine the relationship between culture and cultural production, and the social and economic context in which such production takes place'. But, on the other hand, our critical evaluation of contemporary writing 'may be seen as part of that systematic enterprise of demystification and of tireless ideological analysis which is undoubtedly the most fundamental role which a Marxist criticism or journalism can fulfil for the public at large'. On the one side, then, a study which is scientific, exhaustive, analytic, placing the literary work within the contradictory complexity of relations that constitutes a social formation; but, on the other, a political, discursive, synthetic project aimed at demystification. It is this latter task (rather than the former, to which I do no more than gesture) that I have attempted in this short study of Solzhenitsyn. Now, I do not believe that these different approaches are either mutually exclusive or even separate; on the contrary, it is impossible for one to take place without the other, as if there could be criticism without science or science without a critical

method. But for a study of the present scale and scope I have
found this polarity, nonetheless, to have a certain validity.
Whether I have indeed been systematic or tireless, and whether
I have really succeeded in demystifying anything will, of course,
be for others to judge. But what I certainly have not undertaken
is that total work of historical *explanation* suggested to Jameson
by the study of literature of the past. Rather more narrowly, I
have settled for an attempt at an internal *comprehension* of
Solzhenitsyn's writing. Perhaps this will serve a purpose.

I have used certain words very loosely. Writing, for example,
of 'empiricism' in connection with *One Day in the Life of Ivan
Denisovich,* I do not use this term with philosophical precision to
mean, say, recognition of the absolute validity of sense experience (although that enters into it); but more to indicate a kind
of reticent opacity in the book, a tendency to say 'this is so,
make of it what you will'. I do not think that there is any such
thing as an absolute fact, empirically given, but I am not so sus-
ceptible to the historicist error as to believe that there are not
certain absolute statements which can be made with only minimal irresponsibility. In so far as this is possible, *Ivan Denisovich*
is one of them. It presents us with certain 'facts' of the experience of Stalinism, and does this without comment. Solzhenitsyn does not write here either with approbation or
recrimination; he does not leap to conclusions about the future
or the past of the Soviet Union, but says simply: This happened. This is what I mean by the book's 'empiricism' and
'critical empiricism'. This statement of the particular sense in
which I have used one word is intended to signpost other, perhaps idiosyncratic, usages.

Throughout I have worked from the English translations of
Solzhenitsyn's work, although I am aware of the problems this
creates. The means by which his books have come to be published in the West have sometimes been devious, involving
pirated or corrupt texts, often bearing the accumulated errors
of many *samizdat* typists and of hasty, commercially motivated
translation. To be strict, the object of this study is the Solzhenitsyn of the English language paperback, but then this is also

the Solzhenitsyn who is readily available to a wide English-speaking readership.

What follows is flawed and slight; but that is my fault and does not reflect on those people who have helped me with it. That I have thus squandered their generosity deepens my indebtedness. Father Herbert McCabe, the editor of *New Blackfriars*, will recognise certain passages that are based on articles which first appeared in that journal. I am grateful to him for their initial publication and for permission to use the material here. In the early stages of the work Theo Livinstone patiently shared his knowledge of the Soviet Union with me. Alan Wall gave me constructive criticism and generous encouragement. Elaine Barker made much of it possible. To these and others, for their friendship and assistance, I offer my warmest thanks.

Also two special debts: without my friend and teacher Terry Eagleton neither this nor any other book would ever have been started by me. And without Cathy Given it would never have been finished.

Francis Barker
Ardleigh
26 January 1977

1 Introduction

To follow the development of the writing of Alexander Solzhenitsyn is to record a process; it is to chart the degeneration of a radical opposition to the Soviet bureaucratic regime into an authoritarian moralising. The fierce egalitarianism of the early novels has become obscured by the more widely publicised elitism of Solzhenitsyn's more recent political positions. The double chorus of apologists for state bureaucracy on the one hand and Western bourgeoisie on the other provide an oblique index of this process, rivalling each other in the volume and high pitch of the voices in which they greet each new publication. They begin with a consensus. The appearance of the first short novel *One Day in the Life of Ivan Denisovich* in 1962 marked, for elements then powerful in the Soviet regime, the entry into 'our literature' of 'a powerful talent', 'a true helper . . . in a sacred and vital cause',[1] while for the Western commentator the same book evinced 'powerful realism', it was 'a major artistic accomplishment'. But from these similar starting points divergent courses followed, the Solzhenitsyn of the bourgeois press growing in moral stature, becoming ever more clearly the conscience of Russia, the scourge of Communism, and his counterpart in the language of Soviet officialdom diminishing to a point of infinite baseness as befits a 'renegade who has placed his writings at the service of the darkest forces of imperialist reaction, who has completely alienated himself from the Soviet people and their glorious deeds'.[2] Of course these quotations only reveal the general outline of what were, on both sides of the 'Iron Curtain', more complex trends. In the West reviewers have varied, if not in underlying assumptions, at least in the extent to which their pronouncements have made *explicitly* political use of Solzhenitsyn's work. Lord Home, for

1

example, discerned a harmony between some of Solzhenitsyn's (later) views and various long-cherished fundamentals of British conservative ideology,[3] whereas the Nobel Prize committee has been able to maintain a more 'disinterested', purely literary stance. And on the Soviet side hostile reviews appeared in the press even before the initial acclaim that *Ivan Denisovich* received had died down. Because the initiative was currently with the 'liberalisers', the book's publication constituting the high point of one of the Khrushchevian 'thaws', these first negative reactions were necessarily cautious. Unable to attack the book directly, they adopted a line praising Solzhenitsyn's literary talent but regretting his failure 'to rise to a philosophical perception' of the Stalinist period, by which was meant, as Labedz reports, failure to illustrate the thesis that the Communist Party had still been building socialism during these years despite Stalin's 'errors'.[4] The two orientations, 'for' and 'against' the writer, came to represent in simplified form opposed tendencies within the Soviet leadership, the liberalisers backed up by the unacknowledged support of an increasingly restive intelligentsia arguing for mild reform, while the 'obscurantists' resisted bitterly even the slightest new inroads into ideological orthodoxy and Stalinist norms of state control. With different terms a similar struggle continues today, but in Solzhenitsyn's case the result is well known. The liberalisers gave ground steadily throughout the 'restalinisation' of the sixties and were unable in 1969 to prevent Solzhenitsyn's expulsion from the Writers' Union, and later from the Soviet Union itself. Solzhenitsyn was able to publish little after the first novel, although the first part of *Cancer Ward* went as far as being set up in type by the liberal journal *Novy Mir* whose editor Tvardovsky had fought so hard on Solzhenitsyn's behalf.

Solzhenitsyn's work thus stands at the centre of important political struggles within the Soviet Union, struggles in which the writer himself was at first an apparently unwilling participant, but even this important aspect of his history has been obscured by that larger ideological contest between East and West. But the fact of Solzhenitsyn's alternate fame and notoriety does present an obstacle for the critic. Although the claims of both camps for possession or condemnation of his work are ultimately discountable, they cannot be ignored. It is no new insight to suggest that the extent to which an event is *covered* by the press is directly proportional to the degree of its mystification, but it is an understanding particularly relevant to Soviet affairs. While the 'relative autonomy' of the Soviet press is markedly slight in comparison with the West it is nonetheless 'free' to obey the dictates of its political masters and this is the same freedom which, more subtly, the Western press enjoys. It is not therefore in the pages of *The Times* or of *Pravda* that valuable analysis of Solzhenitsyn's work will be found, but it is necessary to labour against the preconceptions that such organs have already formed. Naturally it is easy for the champions of the 'Free World' to appropriate Solzhenitsyn—in his early work as well as the late—to their own ideological purposes. The demands raised by the 'cultural opposition' in the Soviet Union have the very appearance of liberal demands. The rights of free speech, publication and assembly, for example, the civil rights most cherished of any intelligentsia, when demanded by dissident intellectuals in the Soviet Union are seen to harmonize neatly with the democratic freedoms of the bourgeois West, but do not of course represent the whole picture of Soviet opposition. Widespread and extremely militant working class rebellion in Novocherkask in the same year as Solzhenitsyn's first publication, which followed Khrushchev's announcement of higher meat and dairy prices and included factory occupations and an attack on the local Party headquarters,[5] were not relayed to the Western breakfast table with such alacrity as the 'liberal' demands of a Solzhenitsyn or a Sakharov. Inherent in this selectivity is a concealed and erroneous universalisation of the class structure of Western Europe. The liberal in the West glimpses in the dissident intelligentsia the face of his own class, whereas the militancy of the Soviet working classes he finds understandably repugnant. He misreads and misrepresents the dissident intellectuals. As Harding reminds us, the demand for, say, freedom of speech is by no

means a simply liberal call in the Soviet context; by raising demands which the bureaucracy dare not satisfy the intellectuals
must eventually consider the abolition of the bureaucracy and
the political means by which this may be achieved. Their dissent thus lies 'within the dynamic of permanent revolution'.[6]

Official comment from the other camp must be treated with a
similar distrust. Mandel has described the reactionary dialectic
between Solzhenitsyn and the Soviet bureaucracy. Unable to
counter the writer's arguments, the regime inadvertently
strengthens them by harassment, thereby feeding the writer's
attacks on socialism which in turn enable the bureaucracy to
maintain the fiction that all dissent within the Soviet Union is
right-wing and thus to justify repression.[7]

In order to understand the work of Solzhenitsyn the categories of the Cold War must be rejected. He was no more the
embattled Western liberal who, amid the severities of 'totalita-
rianism', resolutely articulated the values that supposedly
underpin bourgeois democracy, than he is, in a crude way, the
'tool' of American imperialism. It is necessary to analyse his
work as a literature based in the history of a particular society
during a particular phase of its development; a literature complexly overdetermined by the writer's personal history, by the
history of the literary genres within which he works and by the
current political and ideological struggles which form that
literature's genetic environment. Only such an analysis could
render intelligible what the official ideologies of both East and
West have repeatedly obscured. Here, however, a more modest
version of this enormous task is attempted. The following essay
will attempt to chart some of the more important formal and
ideological developments *within* Solzhenitsyn's work. While
such an 'internal' account of his writing would seem to subscribe to the idealist view that literature inhabits some transcendent universal realm above the carpingly rationalistic and
local preoccupations of political analysis, the assumptions that
lie not very far beneath the surface of these unashamedly 'political' rather than 'literary' remarks should serve to emphasise
that the aspects of Solzhenitsyn's work treated here can only be

rendered fully coherent by a far more finished and self-consciously scientific account than is yet possible. This essay thus enacts an orientation towards Solzhenitsyn's work, a *criticism* rather than a fully-fledged *critique*.

Solzhenitsyn's writing can be usefully divided into two periods. The first includes the early novels *One Day in the Life of Ivan Denisovich*, *The First Circle* and *Cancer Ward*. These will be referred to here, for reasons that will become apparent, as the 'democratic' novels. In them Solzhenitsyn is chiefly concerned with the portrayal of Soviet society. These books provide powerful images of that society vitiated by the debilitating effects of Stalinist ideology and interpenetrated and controlled at every level by the coercive apparatus. They are realistic and discursive, combining depiction with the presentation of various ideologies in sharply drawn characters who hold different beliefs and attitudes towards the history of their society which are juxtaposed, and thus silently, but not conclusively, evaluated. The spirit of these books is democratic and sceptical, constantly taking the public ideals of official Soviet ideology and testing them against the perceived reality of Soviet experience. There is a relentless caricaturing of the social elite—the Rusanovs of *Cancer Ward* and the Makarygins of *The First Circle*—which by a process of reduction to absurdity exposes the glibly complacent optimism of orthodoxy. The false democracy of the Stalinist rhetoric and the unctuously hypocritical moral earnestness of the privileged are thrown into clear relief by the long perspective of the labour camps which come, in Solzhenitsyn's work, to represent the characteristic experience of the mass of the people.

The early novels contain many perspectives, differing from the 'ethical socialism' of a Shulubin to the robust but compromised Communist orthodoxy of a Rubin. And while this multiplicity of perspectives may include the most potentially reactionary ideologies—indeed, the populist elements of the early works prefigure the later advocacy of the

'moral simplicity' of Old Russia, a revamped cleri-
calism—such tendencies are restrained by these books'
founding assumption that, as Shulubin puts it, 'history has
rejected capitalism once and for all'.[8] The call for democratisation and ethical reform, although it is limited as will be shown
later, is placed within a socialist context.

The second phase of Solzhenitsyn's writing within the periodisation adopted here includes *August 1914* and *The Gulag Archipelago*, and a series of non-fictional texts of which the most
important are the *Letter to the Fourth Soviet Writers' Congress*, the
Nobel Prize Lecture and the *Letter to Soviet Leaders*. It is in these
texts that a specific ideology defines itself; from the various perspectives available in the 'democratic' novels a determinate
pattern crystallises out. Sceptical juxtaposition with fundamentally anti-Stalinist premises is replaced by a new dogmatism, the content of which—mystical Russian nationalism,
moral and technocratic elitism, and right-wing politics—is
much better known in the West than the earlier, more 'open'
ideology of the first novels. The history of the emergence of this
dogma is an important aspect of the history of Solzhenitsyn's
writing, and this study will attempt to sketch something of this
process of turning away from the realities of Soviet history and
from the possibility of an authentic, socialist, future.

Except under certain very special circumstances any periodisation[9] is bound to have an approximate character, not only
because development never has a smoothly linear evolutionary
shape, but because, on the contrary, each new event in any process is in important ways both a continuation and a new departure. For present purposes, however, certain broad divisions
are necessary, and there are sound historical and political, as
well as literary, reasons for adopting the particular periodisation used here. The first text of the later period, the letter to the
Writers' Congress, written in 1967, marks a turning point, as
Moody suggests, in Solzhenitsyn's personal history.[10] It
was the first of a series of political statements, open letters and
press interviews which attracted much attention within the
Soviet Union and elsewhere. The 1967 letter transformed

Solzhenitsyn's relations with the ruling bureaucracy. It was no longer possible to regard him simply as a writer of increasingly unacceptable novels and stories whom suppression of his work made easy to ignore; Solzhenitsyn became an open political opponent. A steady deterioration in Solzhenitsyn's position led to this crucial juncture. The publication of *One Day in the Life of Ivan Denisovich* was made possible by the active support of Khrushchev, who is said to have wept when it was first read to him. But the marginal cultural freedoms of the 'thaw' were already being dissipated even before Khrushchev's fall in 1964. Solzhenitsyn never again received the Party support and press acclaim of 1962. He was only able to publish four more stories and an article on Russian literary language between 1962 and 1966, and this with increasing difficulty against more and more vociferous opposition. In 1964 he was nominated for a Lenin prize by the editorial board of *Novy Mir* and the Central State Archives of Literature and Art. But the prize went to an altogether safer writer, Oles Gonchar, for the reason that, as *Pravda* tersely announced, 'A. Solzhenitsyn's short novel deserves a positive assessment but it cannot be placed among such outstanding works which are worthy of the Lenin Prize.'[11] It was a further step towards an open break. In 1965 copies of the recently completed *The First Circle*, personal papers, and the only manuscript of a play *The Feast of the Victors*, which Solzhenitsyn has repeatedly repudiated as an immature and unbalanced work, were seized by the KGB; and in 1966 attempts to get *The First Circle* authorised for publication were, of course, unsuccessful. It was against this background that *Novy Mir* endeavoured to publish *Cancer Ward*. The text was submitted to a meeting of the prose section of the Moscow organisation of the Writers' Union. Although there were hostile speakers, the meeting was generally friendly. Speakers offered criticisms of the book and the meeting voted for publication.[12] The first part of the text was set in type but never appeared. At a meeting of the Secretariat of the Writers' Union in September 1967, after Solzhenitsyn's letter to the Congress, opinion was uniformly hostile. It became clear that he would never be able to publish in the Soviet Union without unforeseeable concessions by one side or the other. The publication in the West, despite the writer's clearly expressed opposition, of the early novels did nothing to make publication easier in his own country. While to a certain extent world publicity protected Solzhenitsyn from more extreme forms of reprisal than those he actually suffered, it also made it easy for the Soviet bureaucracy to brand him as an enemy of socialism and of the Soviet Union which, regrettably, in his second, post-1967 period, he increasingly became. Solzhenitsyn's political views became stridently right-wing. The early idea of democracy, inadequate and tentative as it is, gives way to the moralising of the *Letter to Soviet Leaders* with its tirades against Marxism and its forecasts of war with China. And in his literary work of this period the same retrogressive ideology, elements of which were latent in the early work, becomes explicit. But for all this it should be noted, amid the hue and cry on both sides of the Soviet frontier, that a large part of the responsibility for Solzhenitsyn's later extremism lies with the political fear and cultural philistinism of Soviet officialdom who, in trying to suppress the writer, succeeded only in impelling him on a new trajectory towards the ideological and geographical territory of the Western bourgeoisie.

If an important aspect of the internal history of Solzhenitsyn's work is the crystallisation of a specific ideological orientation, a closing of the self-balancing 'debate' which is the formal and ideological structure of the early novels, it is worth outlining, in conclusion to these introductory remarks, some of the terms of this process. *One Day in the Life of Ivan Denisovich* is the point of departure. It is dominated by an empirical and 'valueless' character, and is written in a neutral descriptive style that apparently refuses to judge its content, although valuations are implied by the text. This 'empiricism', the closeness of the book to its material, is of twofold importance: it represents a clean break with previous official 'illustrating literature' and simultaneously reflects central characteristics of Soviet society atomised and depoliticised by the rule of the Stalinist bureaucracy. Both these factors contain the promise of a new and radical Soviet literature, of the repossession of that direct relationship with real history which official writing, with its slavish imitation of accepted models, has effectively concealed. Those reactions to the publication of *Ivan Denisovich* from the literary establishment hostile to the book demonstrate the extent to which even a limited realism was perceived as a threat to the political *status quo*. This is particularly understandable when it is remembered that the Russian novel is traditionally political, and that, in the absence of free debate on political, historical and sociological matters, the writer, albeit covertly, has had to fulfil these tasks. The supporters of Solzhenitsyn perceived equally clearly the implications of the departure that *Ivan Denisovich* represented. The comment of one Soviet writer—'After Solzhenitsyn we cannot write as before'[13]—indicates something of the excitement generated by Solzhentisyn's achievement; and Tvardovsky put the matter a little more articulately when he wrote in his letter to K. Fedin, the man largely responsible for blocking the publication of *Cancer Ward*, 'What matters and is very urgent now is to understand that [Solzhenitsyn] is not at the centre of attention just as himself—however valuable he is in himself—but because owing to complicated circumstances he stands at the crossroads of two opposite trends in our literature—one backward-looking, the other forward-looking and in keeping with the irreversible movement of history.'[14] Tvardovsky senses that Solzhenitsyn's novels represent something *decisive* in the history of Soviet literature.

Yet it is important to notice also the potential dangers of *Ivan Denisovich*'s 'non-evaluative' narrative characteristics. There *are* judgements in the text—a populism centred on the peasant protagonist Shukhov, a belief in the organic goodness of the soil which is revealed when Solzhenitsyn stresses the 'barrenness' of the camp—values which have their basis in a nostalgia for Old Russia. And these judgements, while sufficiently abstract and unemphatic to have no more than a marginal importance in the first book, become more explicit as Solzhenitsyn's work develops, intruding more and more into the 'realism' for which the first book was acclaimed. The logic of *Ivan Denisovich's* empiricism leads eventually to *The Gulag Archipelago*, where, after much development and in different terms, a similar structure—the rehearsal of the terrible 'facts' of Soviet history subsumed under a framework of outmoded value-judgements—is discernible.

The emergence to articulacy of some of the unstated absolutes of *Ivan Denisovich* is a complicated process which will be impossible to trace fully here, but its character may be indicated by an examination of a single idea that occurs throughout Solzhenitsyn's work, in an attempt to demonstrate its evolution and changing implications. The notion that, despite the obvious horror of arbitrary arrest and imprisonment, there are, for some men, some aspects of prison life that are beneficial, is such an idea. It is unnecessary to consider every expression of this idea, it being sufficient to show the difference between its use in the early work and the later. In *The First Circle* it is chiefly Nerzhin who reflects on the advantages of prison life. He recognises that prison has given him certain things he would not have known outside:

> Sometimes he did not regret his five years in jail at all; they had acquired their own kind of validity. Where else but in prison could one get to know people so well, where else could one reflect so well on oneself? It might well be that his unique, preordained consignment to prison had saved him from countless youthful mistakes, from countless false steps.[15]

This is a limited statement of a limited benefit. Nerzhin stresses that it is a description only of his own 'unique' experience and not necessarily a generalisation applicable to all prisoners, and that it is a commentary on prison life to which he subscribes no more than 'sometimes'. While there is, perhaps, a trace of mysticism in the idea of preordination, the two interrogatives are still open to either negative or affirmative responses. The passage tells us more about Nerzhin than it does about prison. Nerzhin amplifies these views later when at his own birthday party, 'carried away by his own eloquence', he makes a speech on the theme of prison friendship:

> I am thirty-one years old. Over these years my life has had its ups and downs, and if it continues on its sinusoidal curve then I may still have my hollow triumphs and moments of imagined greatness; but, I swear I will never forget the real human greatness that I have come to know only in prison![16]

Again the statement is circumscribed, remaining within the limits of the consciousness of the character making it. There is not at this stage the suggestion of a transcendent spiritual quality attaching to the state of captivity, a suggestion which is prominent in *The Gulag Archipelago*. The nearest approach to it in Solzhenitsyn's early work remains within firmly ethical categories and resides chiefly in the belief that the prisoners have a moral advantage over those who remain outside in a state of continual compromise between their consciences and the injustices which they must either subscribe to or ignore. Nerzhin implies this when he says:

> —our lives aren't as bad as all that. Think how fortunate we are to be sitting here round this table, able to exchange ideas without fear or concealment. We couldn't have done that when we were free, could we?[17]

And even here it is a question of fortunate opportunity rather than a qualitatively different moral status.

There is, however, one passage in *The First Circle* where the prison mysticism of *The Gulag Archipelago* is foreshadowed more strongly than in the passages already indicated. This occurs in a lyrical description of the isolation of the prison from the rest of society. The prison is imagined as a ship in the night which 'sailed aimlessly and serenely through that black ocean of human destinies and human folly, casting faint streaks of light from its portholes in its wake'. Continuing the metaphor, the authorial voice describes the condition of the prisoners:

> The men floating in this ark were detached . . . and their thoughts could wander unfettered. They were not hungry and not full. They were not happy and therefore not disturbed by the prospect of forfeiting happiness. Their heads were not full of trivial worries about their jobs, office intrigue or anxieties about promotion, their shoulders unbowed by cares about housing, fuel, food and clothing for their children. Love, man's age-old source of pleasure and suffering, was powerless to touch them with its agony or its expectation . . . From this ark, serenely ploughing its way through the darkness, it was easy for them to survey, as from a great height, the whole tortuous, errant flow of history; yet at the same time, like people completely immersed in it, they could see every pebble in its depths.[18]

At the literal level this passage does not correspond with other aspects of the book's inner world; some of the prisoners are manifestly plagued by anxieties of one kind and another; they do worry about the welfare of their children, and are touched by love. Such information serves to limit (characteristically, in the early novels) the ultimate significance of this passage. At the poetic level, its poignant, elegiac tone and movement, its mythical overtones lulling the reader's awareness of the hardships of prison life, the passage threatens to overstep the limits that *The First Circle* puts upon the root idea of the beneficial aspects of imprisonment; but this remains a threat, and never quite detaches itself from that awareness.

In *The Gulag Archipelago* the same basic idea appears but with very different form and implications. In the later book, the release by deprivation from material anxieties—a hardening of the ascetic equanimity evident in the passage just quoted—has nothing to do with giving the prisoners time to reflect, or the opportunity to make close friendships which would have been impossible outside, but instead it allows 'the prisoner' to enter the 'heavenly kingdom of the liberated spirit', it ushers in a 'dawning enlightenment'. It is no longer the voice of a realistically limited character who perceives that, owing to the peculiarities of his unique personal history, he has derived certain unexpected advantages from prison, but the voice of a seeming omniscience which has begun to make much larger, mystifying claims for the abstract and unspecific 'prisoner' who is thus canonised.

This account of the mutation of a single recurrent idea is offered here as a paradigm of the more general changes in Solzhenitsyn's work. It exemplifies, in schematic form, the broader transitions—from knowledge to belief, from egalitarianism to religious authoritarianism, from the historical fiction of the early novels to the fictional historiography of *The Gulag Archipelago*—transitions certain central features of which the following pages will illustrate.

2 The 'Democratic' Novels

A literary text is both the product of, and a confrontation with, an historical conjuncture, as that conjuncture represents itself in ideology. This somewhat terse formulation is a useful one because it sets the literary critic an important and difficult task, the task of identifying in the text he examines those elements which are 'reflective' of the conjuncture which shaped it, and those elements which stand over against the conjuncture, that make the text discontinuous with, subversive of, the situation that called it into being. And as, of course, these different aspects of the text—its character as historical product and as political activity—are not empirically distinct elements of the text at all, but are, on the contrary, the contradictory 'quality' of the whole text, this gnomic but dialectical formulation forces the critic to examine methods by which the text in its *determinate* specificity nonetheless distantiates itself from its ideological locale. The three major novels of the first period of Solzhenitsyn's development—*One Day in the Life of Ivan Denisovich*, *The First Circle* and *Cancer Ward*—display certain similarities, and a certain evolution of aesthetic form. This internal history is the key to their ideological significance, to their ability to evaluate their own founding ideologies.

Each of these texts shapes itself around a central character, a protagonist who is nevertheless ideologically negative, the antithesis of the 'positive hero' of official realism. The reticent Shukhov, with his unimaginative and severely circumscribed peasant consciousness, and the sceptics Nerzhin and Kostoglotov enact at the centres of 'their' respective novels a certain uncommittedness, an ideological 'openness' which refuses to answer the questions which the novels themselves ask. This is most clearly exemplified by Nerzhin. His enquiry after an

14

ideological orientation which will on the one hand do away with Stalinist dogma while retaining Leninist premises, and on the other make sense of a social history of repression and of Nerzhin's place in that history as a victim, is articulately inconclusive. *The First Circle* records Nerzhin's ideological history from an early break with Stalinism, through a literary nineteenth-century populism and technocratic elitism, to a new populism in which the place of 'the People' is taken by the population of the labour camps. All that remains for the completion of this process, for Nerzhin to arrive at a destination of political and ethical certainty, is the successful conclusion to his prolonged interrogation of the peasant handiman Spiridon, a relationship which Rubin scathingly refers to as Nerzhin 'going among the people' in the fashion of the old Narodniks. But Nerzhin's enquiries founder on Spiridon's enigmatic and bathetic response to Nerzhin's attempt to discover his own philosophical scepticism as the underlying principle of the peasant's rich and diverse experience stoically endured. Spiridon's proverbial wisdom is not translatable into terms which will satisfy Nerzhin, whose intellectual enquiries remain unfinished. This is confirmed and symbolised by Nerzhin's notes on the post-Leninist period of Soviet history. These 'first fruits' upon which he works hard while at the special prison, are burned when he leaves the contemplative realm of Mavrino for the physical struggle of the camps, and yet they are retained in memory; neither completed nor abandoned, they are suspended. Nerzhin's consciousness is thus transitional, questioning but undecided. Scepticism, Nerzhin's own name for the interim nature of his ideas, is no more than a 'roadside shelter where [he] can sit out the bad weather . . . It's a long way of ridding the mind of dogma—that's its value.'[1] But he rejects scepticism as an end in itself, rejects the perpetual ambivalence of programmatic agnosticism. Distressed to hear his own ideas repeated to him by Ruska Doronin, Nerzhin delineates their limitations:

This kind of scepticism, agnosticism, pessimism—whatever

you call it—it all sounds very clever and ruthless, but you must understand that by its very nature it dooms us to futility. It's not a guide to action, and people can't just stand off, so they must have a set of positive beliefs to show them the way.[2]

In the end, Nerzhin knows, active engagement with the object of the sceptic's enquiry must replace the negativity of his stance: the Marxist overtone in the phrase 'guide to action' is significant here. But for Nerzhin the last instance never comes and we do not see beyond his scepticism.

The question that Nerzhin's negativity allows *The First Circle* to ask, and simultaneously ensures that it cannot answer, is 'what should these positive beliefs be?' The book is founded on this question and continually skirts it in the moral and political debates among the uniquely articulate prisoners which the setting of the special prison, gathering a cross-section of the scientific intelligentsia, permits. Tentative answers are offered almost in the margins of the text, implied by dropped remarks and passing references, but when viewed directly they seem to evaporate: Nerzhin quotes to Rubin a Taoist maxim, but when asked if he has become a Taoist Nerzhin's response is characteristic—'I've not decided yet'. A similar function is fulfilled by the suggestion in Nerzhin's conversation with his wife that he has come to believe in a god, but the reference is elusive and disqualified later by Nadya's reflection on the exchange: 'And hadn't he used some peculiar phrase about God? Prison was breaking his spirit, and making an idealist or a mystic of him.'[3] Despite the hints of moral and political certainty at the edges of *The First Circle*, such 'positive beliefs' remain incapable of articulation and Nerzhin's central scepticism, ever on the point of being superseded, is preserved intact.

In *Cancer Ward* the irascible exile Oleg Kostoglotov occupies the negative centre of the book. Like Nerzhin he has a thirst for knowledge but his search is not for the intellectual's pure understanding, it is rather the practical man's need to know. He cajoles the medical student, Zoya, until she lends him

Pathological Anatomy so that he can learn about his own tumour. He needs to understand the theory upon which a treatment is based before he will submit to it. Although he articulates this as a right to the truth, and in this contrasts sharply with Rusanov who in his more frightened moments prefers comforting fictions from the doctors to the 'inhumane' truth, it is as much a reaction to his prison years, a fierce assertion of his independence: 'all my life I've hated being a guinea-pig . . . I must have a look at [the book] and try to work things out . . . For myself.'[4] Kostoglotov has the prisoner's deep distrust of authority. Received opinions are to be treated sceptically because in Kostoglotov's experience they are too often the glib rationalisations of unpleasant facts. He defines intelligence as 'Trusting your eyes but not your ears'.[5] Although his desire for knowledge is a wilful affirmation of his individuality, a determination to think and act for himself in the relative freedom of exile, to take responsibility for himself after the regimentation of the camps, it has a clear political significance. He takes a certain pleasure in offending the pompously orthodox Rusanov, taunting him with ideological heresies and displaying (like Nerzhin) a perverse pride in his status as an outcast, which is to Rusanov an intolerable affront. Kostoglotov's opposition to the dignified self-satisfaction of Rusanov is encapsulated in his approbatory misquotation of Descartes: 'Suspect everything'.[6] This statement, which links Kostoglotov to the more self-conscious philosophical scepticism of Nerzhin (just as his prison cunning links him with Ivan Denisovich Shukhov), expresses in its context his tendency to pontificate when confronted with a willing audience—he is intoxicated by the idea that free men should be listening to *him*—it nonetheless clearly defines his role in the novel as an anti-dogmatist. 'Choosy' and obstinate, he embodies a rejection of the easy solutions of orthodoxy. Such a position is underpinned by *Cancer Ward*'s reiterative emphasis of the historical changes that occur within its time-scheme. Set in February and March 1955, news of the changes in the Supreme Court and of the fall of Malenkov are relayed to the ward on the pages of *Pravda*. News which appalls Rusanov elates Kostoglotov, and his joy is connected with the phrase that recurs, refrain-like, in the book: 'History is on the march'. A sense that the end of the Stalinist period is near (*Cancer Ward* ends with rumours that the exiles will be released before the end of the year) coincides with the book's other recurrent theme of Kostoglotov's return to 'life'. The sensuous spring morning in Tashkent of Kostoglotov's discharge from hospital, the renewal of a personal but representative history, is intertwined with a larger renewal. Kostoglotov's necessarily unpolitical and individualistic scepticism is validated by the novel's sense that the time of the Rusanovs is over.

But Kostoglotov's ideological role does not reach beyond his rejective orientation towards Stalinism. His scepticism coexists with a naive faith in primitive, peasant medicine, and there is at times an apparent—and revealing—incoherence in his characterisation, as if the twin drives towards Nerzhin's articulacy and Shukhov's reticence promote in him an uneasy tension analogous to the fragmented formal arrangement of the work.

Kostoglotov is offered a ready-made ideology by the scholar Shulubin, an ideology identified by some as clearly authorial. He does not, of course, adopt it. At the end of the book his questioning is displaced by the sensuous immersion in Tashkent which gathers up the novel's emphasis on the 'natural' reawakening of Kostoglotov's emotional life and of his sexuality. This displacement of his ethical and political concern, in what is in any case a less discursive novel than *The First Circle*, preserves the 'openness' of the ideological structure, while leaving Shulubin's 'ethical socialism' powerfully resonant, approaching more closely than anything else in the early novels to a 'positive belief' didactically offered. But, characteristically, Shulubin's proposals *are* distanced by the novel, the ending of which is mysterious. Without really knowing why, Kostoglotov decides not to hold either Vera or Zoya to their offers of a bed for the night after his discharge, and he takes the train back to Ush-Terek. He is seized by anguish and the final image is the ambiguous one of Kostoglotov lying prone on the luggage rack with his boots dangling 'toes down over the corridor like a dead man's'.[7] Does he return to the good life in Ush-Terek, images of which, at the very margins of society, his hospital reminiscences of the of Kadmins manage to evoke? Or does he go to his death? The question is unresolved and serves to end the novel on a note of uncertainty just as the Tolstoyan question as to 'what men live by', the focus of ethical debate among the cancer patients, is left without decisive answer. The open-endedness of the novel is emphasised by its last phrases, which recall the senseless cruelty of which Kostoglotov had learned at the zoo; it is stated as an empirical fact without evaluation or comment:

> An evil man threw tobacco in the macaque-rhesus' eyes.
> Just like that . . .[8]

This image, interpreted by some as a symbol of Stalinist repression, is deadpan and opaque; the event happened and its empirical solidity and arbitrariness seem to cancel enquiry or explanation. The book thus ends with an undefined anguish for Kostoglotov and a thought which is unfinishable for itself. As in *The First Circle* where the closing passage, the sports reporter's dispatch, gives a sudden external perspective on the events and debates of the book, placing the novel at a distance from itself, the end of *Cancer Ward* is a final distancing shock of inscrutability.

The type for this final impenetrability, and for the 'negative' central character is Solzhenitsyn's first short novel *One Day in the Life of Ivan Denisovich*. The book stands close to its material incorporating its subject matter, the prisoners' day, into itself as a formal principle. The book offers a temporal fragment in one man's history, a fragment itself subdivided, atomised, punctuated by roll-calls, bells and hooters; the dehistoricised time of the camp, without verticality or development, forms an endless series of discrete events that incessantly repeat themselves. The ordinariness of Shukhov's day is emphasised—'There were three thousand six hundred and fifty-three days like that in his stretch'[9]—and its mild satisfactoriness Shukhov analyses largely in negatives; he hadn't fallen ill, he hadn't been thrown into the lock-up. Written not in a tone of bitter recrimination but in a matter-of-fact, level tone, the book seemingly refuses to evaluate its own content presenting the labour camp as mere *factum brutum* (as Lukács puts it), the necessary premiss of the wily passivity of its negative protagonist Shukhov, who, in a book less formally elaborate than those which succeed it, fills its horizons. It has been pointed out that Shukhov's style and language invade seemingly authorial passages.[10] It is as if he writes his own story, his limited consciousness hardly separable from the 'empirical' structure of the book's form. Within the close limits of this short book, the negative centre *is* the narrative, its reticence belying its totalising capacity. Many have felt that there is a particularly direct relationship between *One Day in the Life of Ivan Denisovich* and the history it is said to depict; Lukács describes this relationship as 'symbolic'. But that history marks the book mainly by its absence. The sketchy accounts of the prisoners' pre-camp existence, usually included to indicate the arbitrary nature of their arrest and imprisonment, and shared memories of the war gesture towards a sense of history which is now missing and from which the prisoners are entirely estranged. Tiurin, as he relates the period of vagrancy that led up to his arrest, 'spoke calmly, *as if he were telling somebody else's story*'.[11] The pragmatic consciousness of the peasant Shukhov, cunning but timid, experienced in camp ways but unadventurous, quick to seize any opportunity but normally cautious, watchful but unreflective, is inextricably tied to the materiality of quotidian existence; it enacts the historical absence of the book's self-sufficient, dense empirical unity. The book's one-dimensionality, its tonal and ideological flatness, those qualities which so offended its orthodox Soviet critics, constitute precisely its aesthetic decisiveness. Breaking sharply with that officially sanctioned writing which Solzhenitsyn refers to, with some justice, as 'cosmetic', the book places at its centre an absence, something which can be implied but not yet said, around which the new literary images of society are organised.

Polyphonic form

Even the external form which Solzhenitsyn seeks for his work bears witness to his message. This form has been termed the polyphonic or horizontal novel. It might equally be described as a story with no chief character. Which is to say that this is not individualism at the expense of the surroundings. Nor may the gallery of persons act as a collective that devours its own constituents, the individuals. Solzhenitsyn has explained what he means in polyphonism: each person becomes the chief character when the action concerns him. This is not just a technique, it is a creed. The narrative focusses on the only human element in existence, the human individual . . .[12]

If, for the moment, the political implications and extravagant sychophancy of tone in this passage are ignored, it does provide a useful description of the larger formal structure of Solzhenitsyn's early novels, the context within which the negative protagonist is placed. Both *The First Circle* and *Cancer Ward* (and to a lesser extent, within finer limits, *One Day in the Life of Ivan Denisovich*) mobilise a broad range of sharply differentiated characters who are made in varying degrees the bearers of historically significant ideologies. The relations between these characters, their debates and disagreements, create tensions between these various world outlooks which are thus balanced and tested against each other and against the practical events of the novels. This 'polyphonic' form, which involves not just the random coexistence of distinct elements as the above quotation implies, but also includes interconnection, parallelism and opposition among the elements, achieves its greatest fluency in *The First Circle*, where the intellectual characters are the most ideologically developed of Solzhenitsyn's cast, giving the novel a discursive as well as a dramatic dimension. The political and ethical positions adopted vary widely from the unstable Communist orthodoxy of the Jewish philologist Rubin who is constantly vexed by the demands of his broader humanism, to the Christianity of Agnia; from Sologdin's idiosyncratic idealist

ethics, to Ruska Doronin's energetic individualism. The variety
of perspectives and the intellectual energy of the prisoners in
itself contrasts distinctively with the lumbering dignity of the
orthodox characters, but the central importance of this formal
arrangement is in its ability to focus an ideological multiplicity
in the restricted environment of the special prison. It thus
organises in microcosmic form that debate prevalent among the
contemporary Soviet intelligentsia about the nature of the good
society and about the future of the Soviet Union in particular.
With the hindsight of Solzhenitsyn's later development it
would be tempting to look here for his own preferences. Indeed
it can be argued from, say, the portrayal of the old Bolshevik
Adamson as an embittered and bad tempered cynic, or the
moral and political capitulation represented by Rubin's collaboration with the prison authorities in his report on prison
security and his work on the recorded telephone message, that
there is a distinct hierarchy of status among the various perspectives.
This hierarchy would reflect the ideological intentionality of
the author. This may be so. But the tendency of the polyphonic
form is in exactly the opposite direction, it works towards the
levelling of different ideologies. The polyphonic form which is
arranged about the negative centre of the sceptical protagonist
ensures an open-endedness in the ideological structure of the
novels. The debate among the prisoners at Mavrino is not con-
cluded just as Nerzhin's movement towards ideological certainty seems to continue beyond the book's final page. This
openness and ideological disperseness checks the tendency in
The First Circle towards explicit endorsement of those ethical
and mystical beliefs which have since become directly indenti-
fied with Solzhenitsyn. Its formal arrangement gives the book
certain meanings *despite* authorial intentionality. The cleri-
calism of Agnia, for example, would be a rich nugget for a critic
interested in discovering a single unambiguous pronouncement
(and as the passage quoted above shows, the search for 'mes-
sages' in fiction continues), but, placed twenty years in the
past, a nostalgic memory that comes to Yakonov at the moment
of his physical and spiritual collapse, it is limited and displaced

from centrality.

This is the significance of the 'polyphonic' form; while it may be open to the liberal-individualistic interpretation cited above, this is only superficial and depends upon a too easy identification of characters in novels with 'the individual' and of the lack of a linear narrative with political liberalism. The importance of polyphony as a *formal structure* is that it *decentres* the novel. It displaces any of the characters and the forms of historical consciousness they articulate from aesthetic centrality. The negative centre is thus installed in a decentred structure the 'positive hero' of which he cannot be.

The specific character of the polyphonic arrangement varies and develops in the three major novels of the early period of Solzhenitsyn's work. *In One Day in the Life of Ivan Denisovich* it appears in its most rudimentary form. In this book, which ironically conforms the most closely of any of Solzhenitsyn's works to the canons of official literary opinion, familiar narrative form—if such a term can aptly be used of *Ivan Denisovich*'s 'empirical' sequentiality—is of far more importance than its embryonic polyphony. The consciousness of the characters is narrow in any case and essentially practical, exemplifying 'ideological consciousness' rather than articulating 'ideologies'. And evaluative assumptions are buried deep beneath the surface of the text and, necessary for the success of the book's descriptive mode, are abstract and absolute. But it is useful, in the light of the later books' more developed ideological multiplicity, to notice in the first text the outlines of the later form. Its treatment, for example, of Christian ideology is characteristically ambiguous. Shukhov occasionally prays but is unconvinced of the value of prayer. He compares it to the judicial appeals that the prisoners are allowed to lodge—they never receive any answers. And he is bitterly anti-clerical:

> In Polomnya, our parish, there isn't a man richer than the priest . . . He pays alimony to three women in three different towns, and he's living with a fourth. And he keeps that bishop of his on a hook, I can tell you. Oh yes, he gives his fat

hand to the bishop, our priest does.[13]

This is typical of the negative consciousness of the protagonist. Based on his experience of one priest, Shukhov's tone is undemonstrative, a spokesman for neither the church nor for militant irreligion, but restricted within the limits of his conservative, peasant characterisation he demonstrates a reticence towards the issue he raises. He rejects the ideas of paradise and hell, and treats the constantly Bible-reading Baptist, Alyosha, with a mixture of suspicion—'those fellows were fond of recruiting'—and grudging admiration: 'Baptists . . . They shed the hardships of camp life like water off a duck's back'.[14] But crucially, the marginal presence of Christianity in the book, ambivalently portrayed as *content* in any case, is *formally* counterbalanced by quite another system of values, as, for instance, when Buinovsky denounces the camp guards who are harassing the prisoners with an unnecessary body-search: 'You're not behaving like Soviet people . . . You're not behaving like Communists.'[15] Alyosha's meekness and resilience is, no doubt, as admirable as Buinovsky's appeal to the guards. Shukhov's 'negativity' admits and fends off both, allowing the entry into the book of two quite different perspectives without aesthetically prioritising either. This exemplifies in simple form the more elaborate polyphony of *The First Circle* and of *Cancer Ward*.

Ideology—forms
The negative protagonist and the polyphonic organisation of these novels enact a tension between two divergent formal tendencies, a tension motivating and motivated by their mutual asymmetry. The aesthetic index of this tension in *The First Circle*, the most elaborately polyphonic of the novels (in *Cancer Ward* the structure simplifies itself again into the central confrontation between Kostoglotov and Rusanov which predominates over the polyphony of minor characters), is the sometimes crude devices which are introduced to impose unity on what would otherwise have been an episodic work. Various

improbable interconnections between different narrative strands, and relationships between characters, serve only to emphasise the problems they try to resolve. That Eva, the student room-mate of Nerzhin's wife, is reading the collected works of Galakhov, the writer who appears later at the Makary-gins' dinner party; that Radovich is an old friend of the prisoner Adamson; that Major Roitman lives in a flat where Nerzhin laid the parquet floors; and numerous other examples, attempt to bind together the potentially centrifugal tendencies of poly-phonic form. These arbitrary devices are necessitated by the in-ability of the negative protagonist to centralise the outward, episodic tendency of the novel's equalised materials. And the tendency towards centralisation, represented by the very pres-ence of a protagonist, is frustrated by the negativity of that centre, the protagonist's failure to totalise the novel's ideology that is ensured by his installation in a formal asymmetry.

These opposite formal tendencies connect with divergent ideological assumptions. Polyphony tends towards the repre-sentation of society as a random agglomeration of 'individuals' with their distinct but adjacent destinies; while the presence in the novel of a protagonist, on the other hand, implies a view that there can be a unifying principle of such accidental, atomic existence, that it can be made coherent by the activity and con-sciousness of a central personality. The two tendencies enact, on the one side, an incorporative dynamic, a movement towards totality, towards organic, rounded organisation, a sense of fictive community, and on the other, a thrust towards fragmentation and atomisation, towards the destruction of community in an individualisation of perspective and ideology. The one is a movement towards formal wholeness, the human-ist unity of bourgeois realism, the other an impulse towards partiality and subjectivism.

If the aesthetic problematic which these novels, by rejection, simultaneously defined and made visible is that of official, opti-mistic literature, with its linear narrative and positive hero (a formal organisation which, with irony, *One Day in the Life of Ivan Denisovich* uses against itself), the ideological conjuncture to which these novels, principally in their formal tensions, allude is that of the post-Stalinist breakdown of monolithic orthodoxy. In the period from which the novels come an increasing awareness of the inability of traditional dogma to solve the problems facing Soviet society, political changes and changes in the state and economic structures (particularly Khrushchev's attempt partly to decentralise the economy), and the need for wider and more versatile discussion, constituted a certain dispersal of monolithism, a certain widening of the parameters of official ideology. Problems such as that of the contradiction between rising living standards and material expectations, and the continued inability of the economy to provide consumer goods, the desperate inefficiency of Soviet industry, necessitated a search for perspectives and solutions which would previously have been outside the margins of personal safety. There have even been calls, for example, for the reintroduction of a market economy. Admittedly such suggestions have not appeared in the pages of *Pravda* but they have nonetheless been expressed in influential circles. The emergence of a dissident intelligentsia, in part inadvertently fostered by sections of the ruling group— as in Khrushchev's promotion of *Ivan Denisovich*—was an important instance of this monolithic breakdown. The 'loyal' oppositionism of the more prominent sections of the dissident intelligentsia, their 'fabian' democratic slogans, represent a tendency towards ideological pluralism which has been accepted, to an extent, in ruling circles. Ticktin, in an important article, emphasises the extent to which the dissident intelligentsia is an 'extreme' version of the incorporated intelligentsia which is materially tied to the ruling group and has, within certain limits, a harmony of interests with that group.[16]

It would be wrong to overestimate the fundamentality of these changes; they (still) represent no more than a *trend* in Soviet social development. It should be remembered that Khrushchev, whose policy towards ideological 'liberalism' contained considerable ambiguity and sharp changes of direction, was deposed by the party less than two years after the publication of *Ivan Denisovich*. And the period following his fall, a

period of steady hardening of the official line on dissidents leading up to the severe repression of intellectuals around 1968, has
been described, with some felicity, as one of 'restalinisation'.
Pluralism, articulated as a principle by sections of the intelligentsia and evidenced by the range of positions put forward by
them (ranging, as Ticktin puts it, from Marxism to slav fascism) has not yet become a decisive feature of ideological life in
the Soviet Union. It is something over which a continuing struggle is fought. And perhaps most important of all, this struggle
takes place upon the ground of Stalinist orthodoxy; opposition
tends to be defined by the orthodoxy it 'loyally' resists. There is
thus a tendency in the ideologies which constitute the *de facto*
pluralism towards the same 'totalitarian' claims as those of the
ideology they combat.

The formal tensions of Solzhenitsyn's early novels, between
centrifugal polyphony and formal centralisation in a protagonist who is nonetheless negative, reproduce the structure of the
works' external ideological problematic. The tendency towards
fragmentation in the episodic polyphonic organisation of the
fiction corresponds to emerging ideological heterodoxy, the
very possibility of polyphony only existing in opposition to the
monistic imperatives of 'socialist realism', the linear narratives
of the Stakhanovite literature, and introducing along with a
new form a new content, the previously unmentioned labour
camp theme. This multiplicity, the incorporation into the text
of a variety of ideological orientations is the index in literary
form of the amorphousness, the 'incoherence' of the first public
re-emergence of critical thought, an incoherence founded on
the heterogeneity of the intelligentsia as a social group. But the
contrary formal tendency towards centralised unity also has its
'social equivalent' in the ideological conjuncture to which
Solzhenitsyn's fiction is attached. It makes articulate both the
totalitarian 'ground' (the ideological hegemony in contradistinction to which pluralism defines itself) and also the necessity, determined by that rejected hegemony, of shaping a newly
comprehensive form of consciousness. It seeks to replace the
seeming all-inclusiveness of the now fragmenting ideological

monolith with a new totalisation, a new perspective capable of posing, explaining and solving the practical problems currently perceived. Yet the very fact that the protagonist, who carries this centralising tendency, is a negative quantity, a practical pragmatist or a sceptic who fends off settled perspective, ensures that this dynamic remains a formal structure unable to issue into content as a dramatised 'positive'. It is only the negativity of the protagonist that can allow the levelling democratisation of perspectives that polyphony entails, and that very negativity, in its formal decentrement, preserves the pluralism which its own existence *as protagonist*, as emotional centre of the work, tends to deny.

This tension between pluralism and centralisation cannot be resolved in literature because it has not yet been resolved in practice. Because this tension manifests itself in the novels as a *formal* tension, they can only make purely formal *attempts* at its resolution. For *One Day in the Life of Ivan Denisovich* this problem is not a severe one, as this is the least polyphonically structured of the novels. Its 'empirical' flatness, its merging of form and content into linearity and preoccupation with a single character, poses this problem only in a subdued form. Because the book's negative centre, Shukhov, entirely fills its horizons, and the elements of ideological pluralism in the book (e.g. Alyosha's Christianity as against Buinovsky's Communist ethics, to which reference has already been made) are largely incidental, the tendency towards atomisation is restricted. That is to say, the book is atomic in its entirety, enacting in its severe limitation, its decisiveness of form and content, a pragmatic unity, the given unity of its content: the 'Day' which it reduplicates in its own form. For *The First Circle*, however, because it is the most polyphonically elaborate of the three novels, the problem is severe. It is therefore forced to adopt clumsy formal devices in order to constrain this tension. The mechanically arbitrary interconnections of character and incident in this novel have already been mentioned. They are an index of the tension they try to resolve, drawing attention to it by their unexpectedness. Less obtrusively the short—three day—time-scheme and the

limited geographical extensiveness, devices carried over into
The First Circle from *One Day in the Life of Ivan Denisovich*, also
contribute to the novel's density and compression which try, in
the face of the social atomisation of the Soviet Union, to impose
on the social image that the book embodies a web-like, interdependent self-sufficiency. This sense of closure, which is present
but less marked in *Cancer Ward*, with its restricted setting but
more extensive time, cannot, however, contain the novel's
unfinished quality: for Nerzhin the book's end is a new beginning, and even the last paragraph of *One Day in the Life of Ivan
Denisovich* emphasises the seemingly endless repetition of the
'day' into the linear future. *Cancer Ward* is less polyphonic than
The First Circle, reducing the ideological multiplicity to the duality of the prominent polarity between Rusanov and Shulubin
who pivot about Kostoglotov, the negative centre. The formal
tension is less extreme because the ideological structure is more
explicit: the book comes near to resorting to the dramatisation
of an ideological 'positive' in Shulubin's 'ethical socialism',
such a positive in part superseding the baroque multiplication
of perspective of *The First Circle*. But Shulubin's ethical proposals, perhaps the ideological centre of the book, are still displaced from the formal centre, and as has already been
suggested are dispersed by the immersion of Kostoglotov in the
'sub-ideological' sensuousness of the Tashkent experience. But
this diffusion of the book's ideological concerns, and the enigma
of Kostoglotov's destiny, *is* the index in *Cancer Ward* of the tension between centralisation and pluralism. Where *The First
Circle* falls back on devices of compression and interconnection,
Cancer Ward tends to dissipate the tension by shifting the book's
setting from the cancer ward, the site of ideological conflict,
into Tashkent where it becomes, like *One Day in the Life of Ivan
Denisovich*, the linear narrative of a single character. Where *The
First Circle* preserves an elaborate polyphony at the expense of
ideological centralisation, *Cancer Ward*, with, in Shulubin, a displaced but firmer ideological certainty, must finally abandon
polyphony.

This formal tension, impossible to adequately resolve, is a

sign that in a sense these books cannot yet be completed. They are necessarily inconclusive in their formal arrangements and enact the 'unfinished', dynamic character of the external ideological conjuncture whose indirect products they are.

Ideology of content

With a negative centre about which revolves an egalitarian polyphony of form, a perpetual act of refusal offering the promise of coherence and snatching it away again, it would be an easy but incorrect assumption to conclude that all in these novels is amorphous and in a state of flux, that a *boundless* multiplicity of perspective swirls around an intangible focal point constantly evading recognition. This view, with its implication that the author could somehow become a kind of *tabula rasa* on which the outline of the books' external problematic inscribes itself in *pure* form, would be to confuse the *tendency* of the formal organisation of the fiction with the specificity of its content. Turning now from the forms of Solzhenitsyn's early work to its ideological content, it can be stated immediately that the specific weights and qualities of the novels' several contents enact a definite orientation towards those contents, an evaluative direction which belies the all-embracing 'liberalism' of the quotation noted above which characterises polyphony as 'creed'. Quite contrary to the uncritical evenness there attributed to the novels, their ideological weighting, exhibited in the first place by their ability to caricature the Stalinists of the Soviet bureaucracy and social elite and in the elusive 'universal morality' which is the ghostly principle of the novels' action, is an *active* element 'in' the books' content striving to sublimate and obscure the polyphony-protagonist tension by the invocation of a 'higher' ideological order.

The early novels' portrayal of Stalinists depends almost entirely on two techniques, caricature and ironic juxtaposition. The passages in *The First Circle* which describe the Makarygins' dinner party are a *tour de force* of satirical writing, encapsulating with economy and sureness of definition the moral cynicism and social vulgarity of the petit bourgeois elite. Makarygin's wife is the archetype of class prejudice and narrow 'consumerist psychology' (as the Soviet Academy of Sciences has it) with her concern for old glassware and status symbols, embarrassed contempt for her provincial school friend and disgust with the difficulty of getting servants 'nowadays'. And Makarygin himself, less egocentric than his wife, inhabits the same self-satisfied *milieu*; his quiet pride in his 'smoker's altar', with which he tries to impress the gross General Slovuta, matching her material triviality. The orgy of slightly drunken luxury into which the dinner party develops is, however, fractured by the introduction into these passages of other material. The 'other realm' of *The First Circle*, prison life, intrudes through the young woman who, with a distasteful lack of tact, petitions the bureaucrat from the Supreme Soviet for the release of her father, dying in a labour camp. And in the story which Makarygin repeats of his daughter Clara's attack on his workerist pretensions, and in Radovich's important invocation of Leninism, his denunciation of the Makarygins' social privilege as 'bourgeois corruption', explicit criticism enters the world of the book's elite. These passages contain therefore two kinds of critique. The first of these is immanent; it is latent in the exaggerating stylisation of the caricaturing mode. The Makarygins and their guests are *figures* drawn out *ad absurdum*. This stylisation opens up a gap between their democratic slogans and the complacent but ruthless self-interest of their social practice. The same kind of critique is latent in the portrayal of the secret police bureaucrat Rusanov ('I'm in personnel') in *Cancer Ward*, and in that of his wife and daughter, Aviette. Social snobbery, a blustering but increasingly insecure assumption of innate superiority, fear of the masses, and an underlying malevolent desire to 'check up on' the doctors and patients of the cancer clinic, coalesce in Rusanov into a parody of orthodoxy, motivated by expediency and condemned finally to extinction. This kind of caricatured depiction of Stalinists is by no means even. The Makarygins and Rusanov represent it in extreme form. In *The First Circle* a range of bureaucratic characters—from Stalin down to Junior-lieutenant Nadelashin—is represented with

varying degrees of stylisation. Yakonov, for example, the chief
engineer at Mavrino, exhibits both Rusanovesque qualities and
also a more 'sympathetic' aspect allowed by his distance from
the political centre. Where the bureaucrats close to Stalin are
tied to the rigidity of a necessary subservience, Yakonov, with a
tainted record, unable to join the Communist Party, is allowed
a certain autonomy of thought and action, which partially
retrieves him from the stylisation of a Rusanov. In Yakonov the
Janus-like relativism of Abakumov—a bully to his subordinates
and a fawning innocent to Stalin—is less extreme. In a similar
way Rubin, forever wracked by the contradiction between his
Communist orthodoxy and the humanism through which he
became a Communist in the first place, exhibits a duality of tex-
ture, a full and rounded character in his humanist aspect but
caricatured in his orthodoxy.

This kind of internal critique of content which undermines
various characters through the mode of their portrayal is supplemented by the technique of ironic juxtaposition which polyphonic organisation allows. Set over against the opulence of the
Makarygins' *milieu* is the material deprivation of the students,
the prisoners' wives—expressed particularly in the letters from
Dyrsin's wife, the pathos heightened by the framework of the
security officer Mishin's bland optimisms—and of the existence of the prisoners themselves. In the contrasts between
these different social levels, in the ironies and discrepancies between them, 'silent' judgements are contained, judgements
never articulated in the books, either by character or narra-
tion, but offering themselves seemingly spontaneously in the
relations between different areas of content.

The second kind of critique of content is the explicit criticism represented by Radovich's Leninism, Clara's ridicule of
her father, and, in *Cancer Ward*, Shulubin's opposition to
Rusanov, and Dyoma's invocation of the sincerity-in-literature
debate against Aviette's literary officialese. As with the caricaturing mode there is considerable unevenness within this range
of critical opposition to portrayed orthodoxy. Any of the critical viewpoints thus introduced could be (and have, by various

critics, been) taken as the novels' 'positives', their definitive 'message' which can be carried away from the text by the reader as a lesson learned. The didacticism of this literary-critical assumption, which abstracts from content ideological proposals, is no longer tenable when it is becoming increasingly clear to criticism that it is everywhere *form*, bearing in its convolutions the imprint of history, that is the 'secret' of content, constraining the text always to mean something other than it explicitly says. In point of fact, the significance of these various critical perspectives is not that they constitute those 'positive beliefs' that *The First Circle* puts on the agenda, or the answer to *Cancer Ward*'s questioning of 'what men live by'; their significance lies, rather, in their *function* as sources of criticism from a wide political spectrum. It is their critical relations, polyphonically deployed, to portrayed Stalinism which gives them objective structural importance for the fiction, and not the subjective selectivity of the critic who may like the look of Agnia's religiosity rather more than Radovich's Bolshevism.

If there is a positive ideological content of these novels it is not an explicit one, but the unobtrusive underside of these various orientations, a structure of gestures towards 'positive beliefs' of which these explicit critical ideologies, in their formal arrangement rather than their portable content, hold out a promise. The ideological structure of the fiction is the structure, made possible by form, of these shades of certainty. Here is the connection between the two modes of internal critique—caricature and ideological dissent. The caricaturing mode may usually be defined as a conservative mode which dramatises the aberrations from confidently assumed norms which, precisely because of their stable self-evidence, need never be alluded to directly. Solzhenitsyn's fiction inverts this customary arrangement, in that the norms implied are not the unspoken fundamentals of an ideological *status quo* but the proposed alternatives to the perceived relativism and expediency of the disintegrating hegemony. The caricaturing mode allows an immanent critique of material, contrasting aims with existence (Stalinist 'democratic' rhetoric against practical self-interest) portraying and evaluating in one moment the content it simultaneously pictures and derides. But this depends upon certain founding assumptions, a certain structure of critical judgements which are silently hinted at by the depiction of deviations from them. These judgements which exist along the margins between the negative protagonist and the perspectives grouped around him, in the unconscious ideological space defined by this formal structure, are, in Solzhenitsyn's fiction, the most universal ethical concepts. This silent content is exhibited unstated, in practical form, in the behaviour (rather than in the consciousness) of the protagonist. They are the underside of his negativity and constitute the ideology *of* the novels.

A quotation from outside the fiction will help to focus this point:

> Justice has been the common patrimony of humanity throughout the ages. It does not cease to exist for the majority even when it is twisted in some ('exclusive') circles. Obviously it is a concept which is inherent in man, since it cannot be traced to any other source. Justice exists even if there are only a few individuals who recognize it as such . . . There is nothing relative about justice, as there is nothing relative about conscience. Indeed, justice *is* conscience, not a personal conscience but the conscience of the whole humanity. Those who clearly recognize the voice of their own conscience usually recognize also the voice of justice.[17]

This passage is, of course, ripe for demystification. Written in October 1967, it stands at the turning point of Solzhenitsyn's work, and already the strident tones of the high moral didacticism of the later Solzhenitsyn can be heard in it. It goes on to voice the irrational epistemology 'as infallible as the internal rhythms of the heart' familiar from *The Gulag Archipelago*, and ends with a snippet of Zionism. But it can be read here, in conjunction with the fiction, as symptomatic of that ethical ideology which lies silently beneath the novels. Noteworthy are the abstractness and claimed universality of the justice-concept (the 'totalitarian' ambitions of the programmatic ideologies of the Soviet 'thaw' have already been referred to), and also its humanism should be recognised. While the concepts of 'conscience' and 'justice' are *ideological* concepts, potentially the objects and not the tools of scientific thought, historically relative and constantly changing their content according to current historical needs as the history of the Soviet Union should amply demonstrate, they can be accepted here as parallels to the literary writing, enjoying a similar (although not identical) 'fictionality' to that of the novels, casting light through their explicitness on the internal ideological problematic of these books of which they are, as it were, the overt self-consciousness.

Lukács—uncritically—brings this problematic to the fore when he writes of *One Day in the Life of Ivan Denisovich* as being founded on the questions 'Who has proved himself [during the Stalinist period] as a human being?' and 'Who has salvaged his human dignity and integrity?'[18] Lukács accepts what is in the end an essentially ethical endorsement of the novels which contents itself with reduplicating in the critical discourse the ethical preoccupations of the artistic one. Such an endeavour is well supported by Solzhenitsyn's own comments on the tasks of the writer:

> It is not the task of the writer to defend or criticise one or another mode of distributing the social product or to defend one or another form of government organisation. The task of the writer is to select more universal, eternal questions [such as] the secrets of the human heart, the triumph over spiritual sorrow, the laws of the history of mankind that were born in the depths of time immemorial and that will cease to exist only when the sun ceases to shine.[19]

The 'more universal, eternal questions . . . secrets . . . triumphs . . . laws' are the covert content of the early novels, which strives, as the underlying assumptions that validate the caricaturing mode and also seek to form the ethical highest common factor of the critical ideologies incorporated polyphonically into the text, to harmonise the contradictions of form through the fundamentality of a universal ethical scheme. The activity of this ethical universalism in the fiction takes various forms. In the pragmatic *One Day in the Life of Ivan Denisovich* it consists in a system of judgements buried deep in the text. It has been suggested above that this text refuses to evaluate its own content, this may now be modified to include certain 'deep' significances. In, for example, one of the book's rare 'total' characterisations of the camp, the most abstract 'critical' category is invoked:

> The steppe was barren and windswept, with a dry wind in summer and a freezing one in winter. Nothing could ever grow in that steppe, less than nothing behind four barriers of barbed wire.[20]

This image which, compounding the arid natural environment with the human harshness of the barbed wire, is both realistically accurate and metaphorical, contains a valuation in its concealed belief in the goodness of the soil and of organic growth. The same idea occurs again in the book in the images of food and of mealtimes as temporal atoms somehow retrieved from the meaninglessness of dehistoricised camp existence. Mealtimes 'belong' to the prisoners who can read the months of the year by the vegetables floating in their gruel, linking them back to the natural order which camp life perpetually negates. In the trivial linearity of camp time it is precisely 'growth' (the abstract, universal positive at work here), in the historical dimension, of which the prisoners are deprived, implying a critical view of Stalinism as an 'artificial' clamping of historical development, imposing bureaucratic strictures on the historically generated patterns of the ongoing revolution.

In the polyphonically complex *Cancer Ward* and *The First Circle* the ethical 'underside' is alluded to by the novels' action. Each sets its characters a test, essentially an ethical one, and judges them according to their success of failure. In *The First*

Circle Nerzhin is faced with the dilemma of Yakonov's offer of work as a cryptanalyst with the possibility of remission and a pardon. But such work would involve active cooperation with the prison authorities and is rejected by him. Nerzhin is not conscious of the ethical basis of his decision; he speaks merely of it being 'time' to go back to the labour camps, which is the direct result of his refusal. This exemplifies the universal ethical schema as the 'subconscious' of the text. Similar dilemmas are faced by Sologdin who also seems to reject the easy course of collaboration by destroying his design of the telephone scrambler, but as it turns out he uses this act only as a bargaining counter with which to win concessions from Yakonov. His eccentric idealist ethics—the 'law of the last inch' and the rest— are thus discredited by his individualistic practice. Similarly Nadya must decide whether to divorce Nerzhin in order to protect her place at the university. And the student Musa is confronted by the contradiction between material pressure and a sense of the wrongness of acquiescence when she becomes the object of KGB threats and inducements to become a police informer. But most instructive is the case of Rubin. For him the moral test is posed by the recorded telephone warning that Volodin attempted to convey to the doctor Dobroumov. He initially warms to the project of identifying the caller's voice patterns as a service to the cause of socialism, but his enthusiasm diminishes when he becomes aware of the nature of the state secret he is being asked to protect. Worried by his belief that medical knowledge is international and not in disclosure a threat to the security of the Soviet Union, he rationalises his continued collaboration as purely scientific interest in the project, allowing his excitement at the prospect of founding a new science of voice-prints to displace the previously-perceived moral issue. He at last gains relief, but not vindication, from Oskulopov's brisk willingness to arrest all the suspects, thus apparently relieving Rubin of the responsibility for effectively condemning any one or two of them.

In *Cancer Ward* the test is sickness and death. Various responses are elicited from the different characters. The dominant polarity is between Rusanov's inner fear, the progressive dissolution of his orthodox optimism, and Kostoglotov's will to survive in independence and self-sufficiency. These two poles are supplemented by other characters' reactions. Vadim's Communist single-mindedness, the driving passion of his geological research, wanes as his resolve weakens with the worsening of his illness. His clear-cut opinions win Rusanov's approval but lack the inner resources to hold out against physical decline. Asya also falls on this side of the dividing line, her promiscuous hedonism unable to prevent hysterical collapse. Dyoma on the other hand, after initial fear of the amputation of his leg, faces the operation and the future courageously and with his plans intact.

The social image which the underlying ethical assumptions promote consists mainly in depicting society as a configuration of discrete individuals, each with absolute personal moral responsibility. Important examples of this are Innokenty Volodin in *The First Circle* and Zotov in the minor work *An Incident at Krechetovka Station*. Zotov is a Nerzhin about to develop. His studious reading of Marx and dedication to duty, his concern for the starving soldiers, form a picture of an ordinary minor official: not a particularly praiseworthy man, but not a Rusanov either. His behaviour towards Tveritinov is similarly unexceptional, initial warmth giving way to what is, for wartime, a justifiable suspicion. But at the last something changes in Zotov. In his tentative enquiries after Tveritinov, for whose arrest he is responsible, and in the troublesome memories of his 'haunting smile' is the germ of a wider consciousness, an unspecific but nagging unease so that 'afterward, for the rest of his life, Zotov could never forget that man . . .'[21] In Volodin the dawning of an ethical sense is explicit. He is transferred during the course of the book from the realm of 'epicurean' Moscow Society, with its comfort, affluence and promise of a successful diplomatic career, to the realm of Gulag, his harsh entry into which, the destruction of his physical and mental composure, the demeaning shedding of clothes, the humiliation of the prison reception routine, preoccupies the long closing sections of *The First Circle*. And at the frontier between these two worlds is Volodin's discovery of his 'conscience'. His initial ethic of 'you only live once', his vulgar materialism enervated by a sated world-weariness, is powerless to combat the idealist moral philosophy of his mother's notebooks which flows into the arid spiritual vacuum of Volodin's orthodoxy. The narrative of Volodin, placed in a significant formal position framing the other contents of the book, is one of the few eruptions into the content of *The First Circle* of the ethical assumptions which otherwise lie silent beneath its action.

This individual-moral ideology helps to explain *The First Circle*'s portrayal of Stalin, in which it meets its aesthetic limitations. The Stalin-figure is artistically problematical, lacking the inner consistency of some of Solzhenitsyn's other characters. The various elements of which the figure is composed— varying from a quasi-tragic pathos to the crude absurdity of Stalin's fantasies, from innocent stupidity to malevolent cunning—are neither interdependent nor do they coexist in the fruitful tension that animates a Rubin, but are simply juxtaposed in the unreconciled existence of a self-consciously literary construct. Although it has been claimed that Solzhenitsyn's Stalin corresponds to all the known facts of the personality of the real historical figure,[22] this claim evades the aesthetic issue: regarded as a character study it leaves enigmatic the core of the personality it purports to portray, an enigma not mysterious but lacking in conviction. Wanting the formal plasticity of the rest of the text, the portrayal of Stalin protrudes from *The First Circle*'s dominant realism and places at the commanding heights of the book's fictional world of interacting characters an excellent and facile cartoon. This artistic inconsistency betrays the limitations of Solzhenitsyn's customary method of understanding and picturing history as the self-activity of individuals. Such an artistic epistemology, when shaping its images of a society hierarchically stratified but nonetheless determined by historical forces greater than the individual, must inevitably seek (in the person of Stalin) an individual prime mover, source and author of his society, but, in the impossibility of so portraying history, is rebuffed by its own premisses. It is necessary to propose a different interpretation of the Stalin figure from the naturalistic explanation which has just been mentioned. The portrayal should be seen as fulfilling a quite different function from that of disclosing the inner life of a real personality. The characteristic and capacities that Solzhenitsyn invests in his Stalin also permeate his picture of the Soviet bureacracy and social elite. The figure is an extreme version of that caricaturing tendency which has already been discussed. In an individualistically portrayed society Solzhenitsyn sees Stalin as one who imparts his own qualities to the rest so that 'Just as King Midas turned everything he touched into gold, so Stalin's touch turned everything into mediocrity.'[23] Stalin's brutal cynicism, his grandiose self-importance and inner emptiness reappear in the other members of the state apparatus that radiates from him. His presence infiltrates the entire novel: it is for him that the work at Mavrino is undertaken, he is present in the prisoners' abuse, in the toasts at the Makarygins' party and in the portrait that dominates Abakumov's office before which Yakonov, Sevatyanov and Oskulopov deferentially lower their eyes. All these signs lead back to the political centre where the caricatured Stalin acts as a prism through which the book focusses its picture of the Soviet regime, encapsulating in exaggerated and distilled form that which the novel, on the ground of its universal ethical underside, rejects.[24]

Politics

The individual-moral problematic of Solzhenitsyn's early work, occasionally coming to explicit statement in the texts and always latent (in practical form) in the activity of certain characters, gives the greatest cause for concern to that argument which sees in these novels a genuinely democratic impulse. Turning now to the political implications of the aspects of his writing that have been considered above there are various problems of interpretation posed. Abstract morality is likely to be distrusted; too often have concepts like 'justice' and 'conscience' been heard in the mouths of ruling class ideologues—

bourgeois and Soviet—where they tend to refer to realities quite opposite to their apparent meanings. And when the obvious-ness of some of these meanings is scrutinised it evaporates, ob-scured by the vagueness of these and other similar categories. Clearly few but the most Rusanovesque of Stalinists would argue that 'loyalty' or 'justice' are undesirable (although he might feign incomprehension or argue, as Rusanov in fact does, that they are irrelevant—'foreign to our way of life'), and this must reflect seriously on the anti-Stalinist purposes for which they are deployed. And the problem of meaning persists. Loyalty to what? Whose justice for whom? These are apposite questions, but questions which Solzhenitsyn's fiction cannot answer, as in the end abstract thought is not the province of literature. Yet even his non-fictional writing of the period leaves quizzical these problems, arguing, for example, that 'in all questions, social or historical (if we are aware of them, not from hearsay or books, but are touched by them spiritually), justice will always suggest a way to act (or judge) . . .'[25] Two examples from the fiction compound the difficulty by offering contradic-tory implications of the universal ethical ideology of the novels. In *The First Circle* there is a noticeable dichotomy, a function of the ideological negativity of the centre, between Nerzhin's in-tellectual investigative role and his role as camp-hardened fighter. When Nerzhin is able to stand up to the prison auth-orities it is not because of his ideological orientation but be-cause of a kind of 'sub-ideological' personal resilience. This may be broken down by the examples of Ruska Doronin and Bobynin, characters in the same novel. The dynamism of the young Ruska, his boundless energy and rich inner life, points beyond the cramping Stalinist orthodoxy, but in the end is de-feated by its own ingenious over-extension and condemned by the self-centred individualism associated with it. In Bobynin, the dour and steadfast engineer, however, different character traits are displayed. Bobynin's innate 'moral superiority' is capable of making Abakumov uneasy and turns Yakonov into an anxious, obsequious colleague. This is a 'given' attribute of Bobynin's personality which identifies him with Nerzhin's ability to resist. Where Solzhenitsyn (half-admiringly) rejects the energies of a Ruska which tend to dangerously overflow all boundaries ('I have the energy of a volcano in me'), threatening order and stability, Nerzhin and Bobynin share a founding inner strength which is an aspect of personality, inherent and received. Although this is modified slightly by Nerzhin's idea of 'the People' as being united by 'character', where there is a suggestion that character can be achieved by personal struggle, these images suggest a dangerously reactionary belief (strengthened by the hindsight of Solzhenitsyn's later work) in innate virtue, in an implied moral elite united and established by nothing more than the apparent accidents of psychology.

Working, however, in the oppositite direction is the example of the confrontation in the story *For the Good of the Cause*[26] between the two Communist Party officials, the careerist area secretary and the benevolent secretary of the town organisation. Again distinguished by personal characteristics—the one has a voice 'like iron girders falling' and the other a kindly manner—they are, however, in this politically explicit but aesthetically inferior work clearly identified not as moral types but as political cyphers, the area man representing the Stalinists and the town secretary who champions the cause of the school students, the Khrushchevian 'new Bolshevik' of the 'thaw'. The town official is doubtless, in the universal ethical scheme, on the side of 'justice', but more significant here is the placing of such an allegiance in a clear political context, the invocation of the ethical ideology in the service of functionaries of a certain limited historical progressiveness.

It is this kind of image which allows an assessment of the political implications of the early novels. It has already been argued that the very universality of the ethical ideology ensures its unobtrusiveness in the text. In *One Day in the Life of Ivan Denisovich* the values under which the empirical image is subsumed are so abstract as to be absent; evaluations are shifted out of the text in order to facilitate the 'non-interpretative' narrative. In the more complexly polyphonic novels the ethical scheme is active only as the unexplicit margin between the negativity of the protagonist and the positive ideologies which his negativity admits but holds at a distance. But in *For the Good of the Cause*, linear novella rather than polyphonic novel, it is dramatised as explicit content with reformist political affiliations. This constrains the *potentially* elitist character of the ideological structure noted above and pushes it back towards an ideological centrism characteristic of (in Deutscher's phrase[27]) the 'fabianism' of the 'loyal opposition'. It suggests the mobilisation of ethical resources for democratic reform.

To define the fragile democratic idea of the early work, so easily able to turn into its opposite in the later writing, is not to discredit it. While it evidently contains the seeds of Solzhenitsyn's later positions, it also marked an important step along the road back from dogma, inevitably difficult and complicated in the Soviet Union. The 'fabians' stand at the turning point in the development of political practice in the Soviet Union; the emergence of revolutionary democracy genuinely inheriting the traditions of 1917 will only be possible on the ground of a newly active working class movement, but the dissent of the intellectuals—constituted often of no more than the most tentative proposals for reform—to whom temporarily, at least, the leadership of the struggle against bureaucracy has passed, must be seen as no more than a contributive but essential moment in that re-emergence. Solzhenitsyn's early fiction gives a powerful voice to that moment. *The First Circle* and *Cancer Ward*, through their ethical ideology, ally themselves with that dissent, but more significantly bear in their formal tensions the imprint of the ideological problematic of which it is but one element. They make that problematic visible by detaching themselves from it. They represent in their contradictory unity the conflict between Stalinist hegemony and new democratic possibilities (as well as, it must be said, less welcome perspectives). In their tendency to fragment they contain the possibility of new paths forward for the Soviet Union, and in the centralising implications of the protagonist, the possibility of a newly coherent view—a possibility which, as the novels in their reticent openness indicate, cannot yet be shaped and portrayed as an historically significant form of consciousness but which can be glimpsed at the edges of the present.

3 After Democracy

The preceding analysis of the literary form of Solzhenitsyn's early novels indicated there an 'openness' corresponding to the fissured and various character of the ideological conjuncture after the at least partial breakdown of monolithic Stalinist orthodoxy. The later period of Solzhenitsyn's work, however, witnesses the solidification in his writing of a specific ideological perspective at odds with the polyphony of the previous fiction. Three more or less directly political texts have been selected here to represent this transition from democratic openness to reactionary closure, and to indicate the main contours of the developed ideology of Solzhenitsyn's post-1967 work: the *Open Letter to the Fourth Soviet Writers' Congress*, the *Nobel Prize Lecture* and the *Letter to Soviet Leaders*.

The *Open Letter*[1] to the Fourth Writers' Congress, held in Moscow in October 1967, overlaps with the 'democratic novels' to the extent that it is an essentially reformist document calling for the removal of abuses and illegalities, and for the implementation of civil rights already largely guaranteed by law, although in practice violated. The first object of the *Open Letter*'s attack is the literary censorship which is unconstitutional and illegal, and which gives bureaucrats who are not literary experts unwarranted control over writers. Innumerable authors have had to make concessions in the form and content of their work in order to pass the censorship; and the works of gifted but unknown writers rarely pass at all. Arbitrary labels like 'ideologically harmful', 'depraved', are used, according to

45

Solzhenitsyn, as sufficient reason for suppressing literary work, but prove to be remarkably fluid: the history of Soviet literature is one of the fluctuating status of authors who are suppressed and then rehabilitated according to the prevailing whim of the controlling authorities. Works at one time 'ideologically harmful' are returned to the Russian people after a delay of twenty or thirty years with their 'errors' explained. Mayakovsky is a useful and striking example. Denounced at one time as 'an anarchist political hooligan' he became overnight one of the Soviet Union's most important poets, a transformation effected by the personal decision of Stalin in the mid-thirties to elevate the poet who had been driven to suicide a few years earlier. Solzhenitsyn cites analogous cases and dryly quotes Pushkin: 'They are capable of loving only the dead.'

But what is most interesting about Solzhenitsyn's opposition to state censorship is the insight it gives into his idea of literary production and distribution. Censorship is, for him, a medieval survival that has managed to prolong its life into the twentieth century and is, in essence, an illegitimate interference into what is properly a 'natural' creative process. It is, for example, 'unfleeting time', and not the agency of men, that separates good books from bad; an impersonal organic process of a kind which will become familiar in *The Gulag Archipelago*. Solzhenitsyn's main argument against censorship is not at root political, nor that of a thinker preoccupied with civil liberty. His concern is for literature, and censorship is repugnant because it inhibits the organic growth of the national literature. There is here, in the subtle but important difference between the constitutional argument and the underlying 'organicist' notion of literary development, the seed of the more mystical notion of the Nation and its Literature which dominates the *Nobel Prize Lecture* and reaches political explicitness in the *Letter to Soviet Leaders*. But so far, in the *Open Letter*, it is only a seed. A balance is preserved between the primary concern for literature to which censorship is seen as an impediment, and the direct and unreserved opposition to censorship in itself, supported by the evidence of a vitiated literature.

The nexus between the criticism of censorship and the notion of an organically developing literature, 'the breath of contemporary society', is provided by Solzhenitsyn's idea of the almost entirely social function of the writer and his work. Soviet censorship has deprived writers of their 'right' to express 'their cautionary judgements about the moral life of man and society' and 'to explain in their own way the social problems and historical experience' of the people. The censorship proscribes or distorts works which might have been expressions of 'the mature thinking of the people, that might have had a timely and salutary influence . . . on the development of a social conscience'. The function of literature is thus both critical and educative, at once an expression of, and guide to, social development. In the neglect of this function both the literature and the society to which it refers are weakened. Soviet literature has lost the 'leading role' it played at the end of the last century and the 'brilliance of experimentation that distinguished it in the 1920s' has been quenched by state control.

The language in which Solzhenitsyn expresses his idea of the social function of literature owes much to the 'ethical universalism' of his early writing. The categories of 'social conscience', of 'threatening moral and social dangers', like many of the juxtaposed ideologies of, say, *The First Circle*, take place upon the same ground as the Stalinism they affect to criticise. There is a curious ambiguity in the *Open Letter* by which many of its statements become simple inversions of officially approved ideas of the social function of literature. While the critical side of Solzhenitsyn's desired literature would hardly please the officials of the state censorship, its educative—basically moral, and possibly moralising—role differs little from their own preconceptions. The demand for the abolition of censorship— formulated at the end of the first section of the *Open Letter* in a proposal for a resolution to the Congress—can be read as an attempt to validate the notion of the socially responsible literature which the censorship supposedly exists in order to ensure. Solzhenitsyn argues that a healthy literature can never be achieved under censorship, but the stated aim is very similar to that of the authorities. In practice, of course, there would be an absolute disagreement between Solzhenitsyn and the authorities over what exactly the 'mature thinking of the people' actually is; but the form of the debate is symmetrical. Hence the legitimacy of describing the *Open Letter* as 'reformist', not only in its political proposals—the abolition of censorship—but in its underlying literary ideology also.

The second section of the letter also ends with a proposed resolution: that guarantees for the defence by the Union of its members against 'slander and unjust prosecution' be written into the Union's statutes. Solzhenitsyn argues that the duties of the Union towards its members are not clearly formulated and that in practice it has never done anything to protect authors' rights. Neither copyright nor freedom of composition and publication is defended by the Union. Slanders in the press and at public meetings have been launched against writers without any right or means of reply, and many authors have been exposed to 'violence and personal persecution'. The Union fails to make its publications open to such writers in order that they may resist these attacks. Even the list of writers who have been expelled or prohibited from joining the Union is not a complete record of those who have been subject to persecution: the number who have disappeared in the camps is unknown.

The third section of the letter presents a list of Solzhenitsyn's personal complaints against the authorities for the suppression, theft or unauthorised circulation of various of his works, and for the prevention of contact with his readership by the banning of public readings of his books. He demands that the Union defend him against these infringements of his rights. The political implications of the *Open Letter* are important for the way in which they accurately characterise the political activity of a section of the dissident intelligentsia. The very idea of an open letter, as a political practice, is deeply 'literary'. It is, of course, impossible to change significantly a state institution like the Writers' Union merely by demanding change. Equally the specific proposals advanced by Solzhenitsyn could never be achieved by letter-writing. The political capital, at best, is made out of the publicity value of the letter (which in this case circulated widely among Soviet writers and literary officials, and provoked comments in sections of the press) and in the very utopianism of the demands. The discrepancy between 'reasonable' minimal demands—validation of what is already 'guaranteed' by law—and the impossibility of their being granted is designed to expose the real underlying nature of the institution itself. Also the open letter serves to provide a focus for dissident opinion: Labedz prints a number of letters from dissident and semi-dissident writers prompted by, and supporting, Solzhenitsyn's own *Open Letter*.[2] But the limits of the political efficacy of this kind of oppositional activity are closely defined by its literary and 'publicist' leaning: no mention is made of the means by which significant change is to be achieved—a limitation which always vitiates Solzhenitsyn's political thinking—and above all the open letter remains the instrument of a reformist intelligentsia that remains tied to what is, literally, dissent, the offering of counter-opinion. While some of the dissident intellectuals have turned, in theory at least, to the Soviet working classes for the key to social change, others—and Solzhenitsyn here exemplifies them—continue to make demands and proposals which must remain unachieved without the underpinning of the political forces and strategy necessary to fulfil them. This kind of individualised dissent, besides betraying a startlingly political naivety (or perhaps a touching faith in the power of argument), turns easily into elitism, a trait already present in the somewhat pontificial tone of the *Open Letter's* pronouncements on the role of literature in society.

Yet despite the deficiencies of the *Open Letter* as a political document, interesting and revealing deficiencies, it serves to represent the character of Solzhenitsyn's political-literary thinking at this point. It falls still within the problematics of the early work, the demand for the regeneration of various forms and ideologies of Soviet society from the cynical disuse into which they have fallen, rather than the fully articulate anti-communist, and anti-Soviet, perspective that succeeds it.

The *Nobel Prize Lecture*, however, takes Solzhenitsyn's literary and political thinking a step beyond the reformist politics of the pre-1967 period, towards substantive attitudes and proposals no longer reconcilable with the basic structure of Soviet society. The direction taken, however, is not that of a radical or revolutionary critique, which must also articulate with the pre-existing situation it seeks to combat, but that of a distinct and separate spiritual ideology which neither offers, nor at times even seeks to offer, plausible solutions to the problems of that society. This is a harsh judgement on a text feted in certain quarters in the West, but a necessary one in view of the dangerous implications of the ideas put forward by it.

Stated synoptically the argument of the *Lecture*[3] is contained in the maxim Solzhenitsyn borrows from Dostoyevsky: 'The world will be served by beauty.' Although by now his language has taken on the self-supporting inner coherence of high moral abstraction, even Solzhenitsyn finds it necessary to offer some explanation of this at first sight less than probable remark. And the explanation lies in a 'theory' of art advanced in the *Lecture* as a prelude to various explicitly political remarks to which the 'non-political' Nobel Prize committee customarily lends itself. Art, in the first place, is ineffable and irrational. It appears like a strange object that a 'primitive savage' finds and fails to understand. We may direct, display and sell art, use it to entertain ourselves but we never thus exhaust its 'original genius'. None of art's *uses* ever fully absorbs the transcendent quality that distinguishes it from other human products.[4] Because of this quality art carries a higher validity than other forms of discourse. The 'whole irrationality of Art' overpowers the operations of mere thought; it is 'too magical to be exhausted by the philosophy of any one artist, by his intellect'.[5] The special quality of art, in short, its beauty, is apparently incompatible with anything but the supra-rational truth, the 'revelations . . . that cannot be explained by rational thought . . . the Inaccessible' for which 'the soul cries out'.[6] So while 'a political speech, a piece of one-sided journalism, a plan for a new social system or a new philosophy . . . can be smoothly and efficiently composed, it seems, on the basis of a mistake or a lie', art, by virtue of its intrinsic beauty will expose the lie. Art bears 'its own checking system' so that 'strained, invented [sic] concepts do not withstand the image test'. The discourse of political or intellectual life *can* be convincingly coherent although founded on wrong premisses—the mistake or the lie—but art touches the heart and, because 'It is useless to state what one's heart does not feel', a truly artistic work is 'completely, irrefutably convincing'.[7]

The aesthetic 'theory' outlined at the beginning of the *Lecture* is one of considerable naivety. While, after the empiricist myopia which seems always to affect academic debate on the subject, it is refreshing to find a writer prepared to make a broad statement about the nature of art, it is impossible to assent to the statements themselves. What is being put forward is an aesthetic mysticism deriving the production and distribution of art from, and assimilating them to, a spiritual 'experience' which is irrational and therefore private, unteachable, and in the strictest sense, unknowable, impossible to understand. Such claims for the ineffability of art abstract it from the world of human society into another more rarified realm of spiritual fiat, beyond reason and, most importantly, beyond discussion. The conservative's dream of the uncontentious calm of an established order is nearly always gratified in aesthetic thought by the removal of the treasured Art from the sordid realm of rational enquiry. When challenged, of course, Solzhenitsyn would not deny rational enquiry, but its subordinate position in his programmatic statements is of great significance. He is not here courting the combative irrationalism of fascism, but the older conservatism that laments the destruction by the bourgeois revolution of the ineffable in favour of the more mechanical operations of the money market. It is no accident that the irrationalism which dominates Solzhenitsyn's writings in their later phase emerges in concert with right-wing political attitudes.

To a mystical aesthetic the *Lecture* adds an empiricist and relativistic epistemology. Because man's 'philosophy of life', it is argued, is 'determined by his experience of life', scales of values are bound to be local and partial. In previous centuries when the world was effectively divided into a large number of separate communities, 'people were unerringly governed by their experience of life in their own limited locality, in their own society, and in the end in their own national territory.[8] And although the norms of social behaviour varied strikingly from society to society it was only 'the occasional traveller' who was surprised by these differences. Within the individual communities, common and workable yardsticks were available to allow decisions to be made about 'what is average, what is unbelievable, what is cruel, what is beyond the bounds of criminal law, what is honesty [and] what is deceit'.[9] Although these standards were based on what was often the 'crooked eye' of experience, they were adequate. But in the middle of the twentieth century, Solzhenitsyn argues, the human race has become united—'reassuringly united and dangerously united'—by international communications and travel. News of events is immediately transmitted from one part of the globe to another but the newspapers and the radio cannot provide the standards by which they should be judged. In this situation the old local standards cannot supply universal norms, and there exists, in a world shrunk by communication, a number of discrepant scales of values. What may seem cruel or unjust in one country is hardly noticed in another, what is nearby is judged differently from what is distant. While it is useless to blame man for this situation—he is by definition an experiential animal—this confusion is dangerous: 'now that the whole human race is squeezed together into a single lump, such mutual misunderstandings threaten it with a swift and stormy end'.[10] What is needed to avoid the apocalypse is a common scale of values, 'one united system of evaluation, for evil deeds and good deeds'.[11] And fortunately there is an agency at hand which can achieve this seemingly impossible task; it can be accomplished by art. The 'miracle' can be achieved because art, and especially literary art, can amplify a person's partial experience by introducing him or her to the experience of another in a concentrated and portable form. In a similar way, despite differences of 'language, custom, and social system', the national experience of one country may be transmitted to another in order that historical mistakes need not be repeated; 'Art can sometimes shorten the dangerous, twisted road of man's history.'[12] The belief articulated here in the re-conciliatory and educative efficacy of art, like Solzhenitsyn's earlier remarks on its truth-bearing properties, is marred and weakened by its superficiality. The initial epistemological as-sumption that 'man' learns, and forms his values, by direct ex-perience, is facile. It represents a wish rather than an analysis. It takes no account of the complex mechanisms (among them precisely 'language, custom and social system') present in any society—be it never so nostalgically pre-technological—for the production and reproduction of social ideology. This extension of some sort of plain man's wisdom to the level of social con-sciousness reveals more about Solzhenitsyn's preoccupations than it does about the creation of actual value-systems. The notion of old communities with settled and common systems of ideas is, in relation to the real history of class-divided societies, no more than a conservative idyll, a retrospective longing for a mythical concensus that can displace actual conflict.

A similar naive, but by no means innocent, simplicity informs Solzhenitsyn's conviction of the effectivity of literature as a means of achieving his desired universal evaluative stan-dards. But a member of Soviet society, before all people, should be aware that the transmission and ideological appropriation of literature is not in the least respect analogous to the acquisition of simple experience by an individual (which is itself, in any case, a deeply ideological activity). In the Soviet Union, as in the West, the press, the schools and universities, the publishing houses, the various forms of censorship, and ultimately the police all serve to process and assimilate literature to the society and the dominant ideology receiving it. While a case may be made out for the critical and even potentially revolutionary effectiveness of important art, it is blindness to ignore, as Solz-henitsyn does, the material, social forces at work in the cultural transactions of any recognisably real world. Refusing, as all ('philosophical') idealists do, to acknowledge that systems of ideas and values, and even literature itself, are rooted in a contradictory social reality, and cannot, transcendent, evade the real conditions of their production, distribution and exchange, Solzhenitsyn turns away from the real world towards one of his own making.

The *Nobel Prize Lecture* displays within its aesthetic remarks a political and ideological orientation of a markedly illiberal kind. In the description of the modern world situation the tones of conservative authoritarianism are dominant. Characteristic of Solzhenitsyn's political 'analyses', his account of the problems facing the world takes as its starting point a literary allusion: the 'devils' of Dostoyevsky's *The Possessed*, once no more than 'figures in a horrible nineteenth-century provincial fantasy', are now 'spreading over the earth'. Hijacking aeroplanes and causing 'fires and explosions', their purpose is to 'shake out and destroy civilisation'.[13] Solzhenitsyn foresees the probable destruction of Western society at the hands of a violence that 'strides naked and victorious over the earth', a 'snarling barbarism' at which 'the entire civilised world trembled'.[14] The sweeping scale of the vision (reminiscent, incidentally, of the language of official Soviet pronouncements—'the entire civilised world . . .') does not exclude attention to the particular detail. With dismissive contempt the young are described as 'those knife-brandishing pirates' who take as an example 'the degrading phenomenon of the Chinese Red Guards' and with no experience of life other than sex are 'blissfully repeating the discredited platitudes of our Russian nineteenth century'.[15] The response of the 'civilised world' to this onslaught has been, in Solzhenitsyn's view, no more than cowardly appeasement. 'The spirit of Munich' which is 'an illness of the willpower of rich people' anxious to put off the day of coming austerity, has everywhere made smiling concessions. Fear of being labelled 'conservative'—a fear which causes Solzhenitsyn little anxiety—has led the people of the West to capitulate to violence and to become, again in Dostoyevsky's words, 'slave to silly little progressive ideas'. Solzhenitsyn calls for an end to the desire for material well-being at the price of increasing instability, and in a ranting passage which surely would have given rise to not a little embarrassment at the customarily lavish Nobel Prize banquet, had the speech ever been delivered, he denounces the willingness to put off the defence of civilisation until later: 'But it won't be all right! The price you have to pay for your cowardice will be all the worse. Courage and victory come to us only when we resign ourselves to making sacrifices.'[16]

The vision of the world expressed in these sections of the *Lecture* demands little comment. Neither a political analysis nor a credible account of the global situation—which is a vacuous abstraction in any case—it is the hysteria of a by now profoundly conservative mind railing against everything—vaguely perceived, Red Guards merging into urban guerillas—as threatening the overriding dream of law and order. Emotional and high pitched, the tirade is as opposed to a complacent bourgeoisie as it is to the movements of the revolutionary left. The call for austerity is symptomatic: although, paradoxically, perceptive in view of the economic crisis currently wracking Western capitalism, it is a familiar adjunct to the more Spartan forms of militant reaction. Not so much an effect of economic conditions, a demand for the customary bourgeois strategy of depressed living standards designed to protect profitability, as a desired antidote to what Solzhenitsyn regards as the effete compromises of the world's ruling classes.

Counter to the vision of conflict and compromise, the central emotional thrust of the *Lecture* is towards a mystified idea of transcendent unity. Solzhenitsyn displays a magisterial distaste for what he sees as the struggle of petty sectional interests. In his view 'caveman impulses' promise to 'tear and rip our world apart' although they have been dignified with 'such "decent" labels as class conflict, race war, the struggle of the masses or the trade unions'.[17] Real material conflicts are seen by Solzhenitsyn—in part reacting, no doubt, against

the degeneration of Marxist language into the familiar Stalinist rhetoric—as no more than the effects of 'greed, envy,
lack of restraint, mutual ill will'; and they should be immediately subsumed, by way of moral reform, under higher spiritual
unity. To this end writers[18] should not stand outside the
world—Solzhenitsyn prides himself that Russian literature has
always acknowledged its 'duty' to its people—but should go
into battle in the name of 'truth'. The writer is implicated in all
the evil done in and by his country, but, although he has no
'weapons of death' it is his responsibility to attack both violence
and complacency, in the name of that overarching unity which
will be represented in a world literature that is 'one great heart
beating in response to the cares and troubles of the world', even
although, Solzhenitsyn adds grudgingly, 'these are seen and
presented in a different way in every different country'.[19] Once
more the idea of a self-evident truth existing over against the
actual world (rather than negotiated with and derived from the
reality of that world) leads Solzhenitsyn towards an idealist
mysticism.

   This last tendency is most clearly evident in those passages of
the *Lecture* that evince the spiritual nationalism later to become
more pronounced in the *Letter to Soviet Leaders*. The phrase 'the
national interest' is one familiar in British political language; it
is used broadly as a slogan of the imposition of ruling class interests upon those of other classes, but in an ideological form,
inherited from traditional Conservatism, seemingly above the
squalid practices of party politics; bourgeois in moment but
aristocratic in form. Solzhenitsyn's idea of the nation and its
literature inhabits a similar ideological space. The writers who
are to be the elite of his moral crusade (we need no longer look
for democratic proposals in Solzhenitsyn's writing) are to
oppose violence by way of exposing 'the lie' which is the principle, according to him, of the violent method of achieving
social or political ends. The lie, it is argued, cannot stand up to
art and thus it and violence will become 'senile' and collapse.
But this abstract task will not be achieved by any mean fac-
tionalism on the writer's part. He must reject the divisiveness of

the different 'parties, movements, castes and groups' in favour
of the truly national perspective with which it is the writer's
duty to commune. He must above all 'give expression to the
national language, which is a nation's main binding force' and
'to the land on which his fellow-countrymen live, and in a few
happy instances . . . also [to] the nation's soul'.[20] The extent of
this turn to the mystical and away from the practical demand
for civil rights of the *Letter to the Fourth Writers' Congress* is tellingly illustrated by Solzhenitsyn's remark that the inter-
ruption by force of the nation's literature (he is thinking of the
writer lost in the prison camps) is no mere 'violation of "freedom of the press"' but 'a shutter across the national heart, an
excision of the national memory'. A country thus afflicted loses
its 'spiritual unity'. Where once the reformist demand for an
abolition of censorship and for freedom of publication placed
the social commitment of the writer within clear, if limited,
political and ideological limits, recognisably relevant to the
changes desired by dissident intellectuals in the Soviet Union,
now the writer's function becomes a near-priestly guardianship
of the sublimated essence of the society suffused with an
olympian contempt for mere politics. This is of course a deeply
political attitude and one that places Solzhenitsyn on the side
of the most reactionary forces at work in contemporary social
conflict. Nationalism is always and everywhere a *bourgeois*
ideology and none the less so for the fact that it is a major part
of Soviet orthodoxy. That the version of nationalism Solzhenitsyn defends in the *Lecture* is a peculiarly spiritualised
one does nothing to weaken this retrograde political implication.

The revulsion from any form of democracy is now complete.
The sublimation of conflict under an ideal of spiritual nation-
hood is no more than a thin gloss on a simple authoritarianism
which throughout the world is seeking to impose—and in some
places, like Chile, succeeding in imposing—more *practical* forms
of national 'unity' in the name of the 'higher', less tangible version. Solzhenitsyn's widely publicised views serve to support
and ratify oppressive movements of the right and he himself

now plays the part of ideologue of reaction, a role to which the *Nobel Prize Lecture* is important testimony.

This sketch of the post-1967 ideology can be completed with a short account of the *Letter to Soviet Leaders*[21] which, as well as making overt the authoritarianism and strident anti-Communism that have already been outlined, introduces to Solzhenitsyn's thought a backward-looking economic primitivism.

The document is Solzhenitsyn's single most important attempt to construct a coherent perspective for the immediate future (measured in decades), both analysing the problems faced by Soviet society and proposing solutions. The two major problems are, in his view, the imminence of war with China and the destruction of Western Civilisation (again the grand abstraction) by economic and technological disaster. But, fortunately, there is a single solution at hand: the jettison of Marxist 'ideology' in favour of a truly national policy which will involve, among other things, the opening up of the so far unexploited Russian North-East.

Initially Solzhenitsyn describes the remarkable successes of Soviet foreign policy, apparently without irony. He regards the transformation of backward Russia into a 'super-power' and the simultaneous decline of the European powers as something that would have been impossible to predict even as late as the entry of the Soviet Union into the Second World War. No one could have foretold the rise in importance of the East nor that the victorious countries in Europe would become exhausted and demoralised by the war and the effort of post-war reconstruction, nor that the United States which had become the 'provider of mankind' would lose to a tiny and distant Asian country, Vietnam. The global picture is, as usual, impressionistic and imprecise. Because of the successes of foreign policy, he argues, and because he addresses in the Soviet leaders 'total realists' Solzhenitsyn does not expect his warnings to be heeded. Only the very wise, he says, listen to advice at the pinnacle of their success if it urges a change of course. Nevertheless Soviet foreign policy has had two notable failures, it bred the Wehrmacht as an enemy for the last war, and China for the next. According to Solzhenitsyn, nobody in the world threatens the Soviet Union other than China, and this approaching war will be fought partly for control of Siberia which the pressure of China's expansion will challenge and partly for 'ideology', for rivalry in the leadership of the world Communist movement and in the interpretation of the 'sacred truth' of the 'Progressive World-View'. If ideology is abandoned this rivalry—by far the more important of the two causes of the foreseen war—will disappear and with it will go not only the threat of war between Communist 'super-powers' but also, revealing the manipulative nature of Solzhenitsyn's account of historical events, various smaller conflicts in other parts of the world sponsored by those powers. The implication is that conspiracy in Moscow and Peking of itself brings oppressed peoples in the 'Third World' into anti-imperialist struggles. All idealists believe that everything flows from ideology and Solzhenitsyn is no exception.

In offering a solution Solzhenitsyn points out, with some accuracy, that in the last war Stalin was more than prepared to set aside any vestige of Marxism in favour of Russian patriotism, and that now the same thing is not only possible but desirable in order not to win a war but to avoid it. And the war must be avoided because, with characteristically apocalyptic extremism, Solzhenitsyn predicts that war with China will be the last in a long series of 'extirpations' of the Russian people with the result, this time, that they 'will virtually cease to exist on this planet'.[22]

The second part of Solzhenitsyn's prognosis—the physiological metaphor is not inappropriate in view of his own tendency to speak of 'the world' and 'the human race' in organic terms—is prefaced by an account of what he calls 'the multiple impasse in which Western civilisation . . . finds itself'.[23] This historical crisis is not simply the result of an 'irresistible, persistent Soviet foreign policy' but is rather the result of an inner crisis—'historical, psychological and moral'—affecting 'the entire culture and world outlook which were conceived at the time of the Renaissance and attained the acme of their expression with the eighteenth-century Enlightenment';[24] which is to say, significantly, that it is a crisis of, precisely, *bourgeois* society: the periodisation is telling. While a full analysis of this crisis is, tantalisingly, 'beyond the scope of this letter', Solzhenitsyn does investigate one aspect of it, which is what he sees as the end of the viability of the idea and reality of *progress*. He means specifically but not exclusively economic progress.

Citing as his authorities the Teilhard de Chardin Society and the Club of Rome, Solzhenitsyn prophesies no less than the extinction of human life on this planet between the years 2020 and 2070. According to these 'scientists' all courses based on economic growth lead to disaster through the exhaustion of natural resources or the total pollution of the 'biosphere'. In the face of this, society must cease to look on the idea of progress as something desirable (a significant widening of the supposedly technical argument) and must instead gear its technology to a 'zero-growth economy'. The West, Solzhenitsyn believes, because it is 'so dynamic and so inventive' will probably be able to avert the catastrophe, and there is still time for the 'Third World' not to follow the Western path (which Solzhenitsyn somewhat confusedly characterises as 'bourgeois-industrial and Marxist'), but Russia, with its 'unwieldiness and . . . inertia' is doomed unless it abandons 'ideology'.

The quality of the economic analysis, meagre and superficial as it is, is less important than the ideological values concealed within it. Its forecasts, for example, are based on the study of five 'factors': population, natural resources, agricultural production, industry and environmental pollution. In common with all bourgeois technical analyses the missing 'factor' is politics. The assumption is that historical development may be understood as a mechanistic interplay of technical processes that operate independently of the social and economic organisation of the countries involved. Nothing is said of the wastage of wealth and resources through the anarchic effects of market forces and profit-guided production, nor of the fact that social wealth in every country in the world, to varying degrees, is appropriated by the few at the expense of the majority, nor of the uneven global and social distribution of the power to make decisions affecting development. The advocacy of a 'zero-growth economy' is an irrelevance—neither desirable nor undesirable, merely off the point—but significant here in that it provides a pseudo-scientific rationale for attacking not just economic growth, but, in the name of 'stability', the conservative's shibboleth, the idea of social development in general. To abandon any attempt to expand production on a global scale and to ignore the possibility of its rational reorganisation, is to argue for the perpetuation of the poverty and social backwardness that is inflicted on large areas of the world including, despite Solzhenitsyn's dangerously idealised view of the advanced capitalist societies, the imperialist heartlands themselves. An argument on its surface concerned with pollution in effect serves to ratify the social relations of production already sustained by existing economies.

And beneath the merely conservative level of Solzhenitsyn's proposal is another layer in which is secreted an ideology not simply of non-development but of return to an earlier, more primitive phase of history. The vision of the stable, growthless society that he urges the Soviet leaders to build in the North-East owes much to a nostalgia for a Russia that no longer exists, and, as with all nostalgia, partial and selective in its programmed reminiscences, never did. Industrial development has 'dirtied and defiled the wide Russian spaces and disfigured the heart of Russia, our beloved Moscow'.[25] But in retaliation Solzhenitsyn invokes the memory of the 'Slavophiles' ('the simpletons never managed to think up another name for themselves') 'who called upon us to cherish and have pity on our past, even on the most god-forsaken hamlet with a couple of hovels'. He associates himself with 'men who said that it was perfectly feasible for . . . Russia, with all its spiritual peculiarities and folk traditions, to find its own particular path'.[26] A suggestion of what this 'path' might be is offered in Solzhenitsyn's advice to the 'Third World' which, still safely on the threshold of industrialisation, 'can only be saved by "small-scale technology" which requires an increase, not a reduction, in manual labour, uses the simplest of machinery, and is based purely on local materials'.[27] The images of a pastoral, petit-bourgeois society of peasants and small artisans, described by Marx succinctly as 'rural idiocy', saturated with a picturesque aura of Old Russia. Attacking 'our "ideological agriculture"' (the collective farms), Solzhenitsyn laments 'the village', which was 'for centuries the mainstay of Russia' but is now 'its chief weakness'.[28]

Although the countryside—to which after the 'sickening roar of aerial armadas' is to be returned a healthy *silence*—is the emotional centre of Solzhenitsyn's proposals, retrieval of the past is not to be confined there. The towns also are to be replaced or remodelled along archaic lines. Contemporary urban life is 'utterly unnatural', but the leaders he addresses are

> all old enough to remember our old towns—towns made for people, horses, dogs—and the trams too; towns which were humane, friendly, cosy places, where the air was always clean, which were snow-clad in winter and in spring redolent with garden aromas streaming through the fences into the streets.[29]

The childhood memory is to be reconstructed in '*new* towns of the *old* type' from which 'poisonous internal combustion engines' are to be prohibited in favour of horses![30]

Arguments against the pollution of the countryside and the dehumanising effects of modern cities enjoy much currency today, but are usually weakened by their one-sidedness. They fail to take into account the political and economic constraints which currently *prevent* the combination of modern industrial techniques with a proper respect for the environment. Such arguments which remain at the level of ecological anxiety alone, and neglect to generate a critique of the political and social organisation which *necessarily* produces the effects they 'lament', are doomed to be no more than impotent protest crying in the face of forces they do not understand. In the absence of the *political* argument for the rational use of technology, and an awareness of the depth and character of the social revolution the attainment of this would demand, their cause grows over into an irrelevant attempt to turn back time, to destroy the real material advances which have been made by modern society. This is the case with Solzhenitsyn's proposals. The demand for simple machinery and an increase in manual labour is an odious call for the continuation, and return to older forms, of the manual slavery which modern techniques, properly used, could end. But what is most important in the proposals is the ideological value of the images of the desired society. A sentimentalised combination of the nineteenth-century Russian countryside and the provincial towns of the first decades of the twentieth are a powerful focus for the traditionalist nostalgia—connected with spiritual nationalism—that inspires the specific measures put forward. The vision, naturally, excludes the darker sides of the old forms it invokes. The slavery of the countryside, its oppressive class structure, and the misery of the urban poor whose quarters were not (and are still not) 'redolent with garden aromas' are tacitly omitted from the images of the healthy society which are built, as Solzhenitsyn says of Soviet industry, 'on ideology'; in this case an ideology of pastoral reaction.

The return to an Old Russia demands, naturally, its patriarchal authority, to be provided in the last analysis by an adaptation of the existing Soviet state apparatus in the direction of *'kindheartedness'*.[31] But the political emphases of the *Letter to Soviet Leaders* are by no means monovalent: two persuasions—bourgeois parliamentarianism and an older, feudalistic authoritarianism—are negotiated uneasily with each other. The former is wanly acknowledged as desirable, but the latter is necessary. Beginning from an axiomatic rejection of all revolutions, Solzhenitsyn looks for a direction in which gradualist change may take place. He argues that there is no significant democratic tradition available and that 'here in Russia, *for sheer lack of practice*, democracy survived for only eight months'. The reference is to the (bourgeois) provisional governments of February to October 1917, and the 'explanation' of their failure is facile. The Cadets and Social Democrats created 'a chaotic caricature of democracy' for which they, and Russia, were 'ill-prepared'. As such elusive preparedness can only have diminished since then, any re-introduction of democracy—defined in *liberal* terms as 'a multi-party parliamentary system'—would now be 'merely . . . a melancholy repetition of 1917'.[32] Alongside his rather pallid advocacy of parliamentarianism in principle, Solzhenitsyn betrays an evident distaste for the system: under parliamentary democracy in many instances 'a fatal course of action' may be chosen as the result of 'self-deception' or of the swing of a small party between two big ones which does not express 'the will of the majority', which is itself, in any case, 'not immune to misdirection'. Further, 'there are very many instances today of groups of workers who have learned to grab as much as they can for themselves . . . And even the most respected democracies have turned out to be powerless against a handful of miserable terrorists.'[33] Clearly even bourgeois democracy is too prone to instability for it to attract Solzhenitsyn's enthusiastic endorsement, although he supports the *idea* (and the class relations that go with it).

It is not, therefore, with much reluctance that Solzhenitsyn settles for an authoritarian regime in the Soviet Union. Compared with the weakness of the democratic tradition, there is an history of authoritarian rule in Russia of a thousand years' duration, which (in one of Solzhenitsyn's most startlingly grotesque judgements) had left 'intact', at the beginning of the twentieth century, 'the physical and spiritual health of her people'.[34] The basis of this judgement—and also the secret of his affective, rather than merely practical, preference for authoritarianism over 'democracy'—is Solzhenitsyn's belief that 'that authoritarian order possessed a strong moral foundation . . . not the ideology of universal violence but Christian Orthodoxy'.[35]

The only question facing Russia, then, is of '*what sort* of authoritarian order lies in store for . . . the future'.[36] Basing his theory on a remarkable assumption of benevolence in the authorities Solzhenitsyn proposes a number of changes in the state structure, familiar, paradoxically, from the 'liberal' democracies of the West. Separation of the legislative, executive and judicial apparatuses is advocated, along with the granting of various civil liberties like freedom of publication and of religious worship and education. A ('de-ideologised') Communist Party will remain in existence, but membership will no longer be a *sine qua non* of state employment and promotion. The only quasi-democratic element in the scheme is a vaguely defined resurrection of the soviets which will facilitate 'consultation' with working people. And of course, Marxism must be abandoned. Solzhenitsyn devotes an entire section of the *Letter to Soviet Leaders* to 'Ideology', in which he ranges alongside more or less trivial attacks upon Marxism (citing, for example, its 'failure' to predict events with the precision of computers . . .), a richly ironic passage in which he argues that removal of state support from Marxism would free 'the numerous people who work in *agitprop* . . . from all possible insulting accusations of self-interest and give them for the first time the opportunity to prove the true strength of their ideological convictions and sincerity'.[37] Again it is the ideological subtext of the remarks that is more important than the surface tirade: the *fact* of Solzhenitsyn's virulent anti-Marxism, in contrast to the position of the early novels, is more significant for his ideological development than is the character of the attack itself, which is little more than an abusive impressionism[38] directed, in any case, at that particular degenerate form of official 'Marxism' current in the Soviet Union.

In subsequent discussion of *The Gulag Archipelago* an attempt will be made to situate the developed ideology of Solzhenitsyn's later work within the differential history of the Soviet intelligentsia. For the moment the present account serves two purposes: to indicate the nature of the transition in Solzhenitsyn's work, and the complexity of the ideological formation which results.

The changing relationship between Solzhenitsyn and the Soviet authorities, and the altering political and ideological situation of the late sixties are not *of themselves* enough to explain the changeover from exploratory realism to dogmatic reaction. It is necessary to discover the internal links, with which this study is chiefly concerned, between the two kinds of perspective. It is no part of the argument that there is an absolute break between discrete positions, but rather that the seeds of the later politics are to be found in the early fiction, and that they *necessitate* the later ideology, given that Solzhenitsyn's work did not develop in the direction of radical democracy because of the external conditions. As has been suggested above, in so far as the early novels put forward a substantive ideological perspective—as distinct from the 'silent', and not necessarily intended, implications of their formal arrangement—it is one of *ethical* mobilisation designed to reinvigorate the stated ideals of Soviet official life with corresponding real practices. The *caricaturing* criticism of Stalinism, for example, is a negative criticism less concerned with a *critique* of its object than an exposure of the gap between appearance and practical actuality. It is within that ethical universalism that the beginnings of the authoritarian moralising of the *Nobel Prize Lecture* can be detected. The insecure and idealist character of the democratic idea of the early work, in the place of a thoroughgoing materialist critique of Soviet society, is vulnerable to mutation in the direction of authoritarianism because, in placing *ideology* at the centre of everything—and ignoring the material forces which determine and produce ideology—it falls prey to the illusion that a 'change of heart' is enough to transform a society. The absurdly idealist character of the *Letter to Soviet Leaders* bears this out, in its proposals (that Soviet 'Marxism' should be simply jettisoned, as if, say, Britain should abandon bourgeois-liberal ideology by a simple decision so to do), and in its form (written originally as a *private* letter of advice).

It is also important at this stage to notice the *complexity* of the structure of Solzhenitsyn's later work, which, while it is indeed

'closed' in the sense that it is underpinned by a sub-text of monistic, anti-democratic fiats, is also extremely mixed. It is constructed of a number of elements of widely different origins.
The easy decision to assign Solzhenitsyn's anti-communism to
the category of 'bourgeois ideology'—as was the case with
many responses from the left—is, as usual, too mechanistic.
Such a judgement fails to recognise the fact that *bourgeois* ideology is itself heterogeneous; traditionalist conservatism may
coexist, or come into conflict with, liberal-technocratic elements, to name but two of the vast but determinate number of
ideological sub-ensembles that may exist in a given historical
conjuncture. Also analysis must take into account the historical
weakness of the bourgeoisie in Russia by which it is far more
likely for anti-communist reaction to reach back for pre-
bourgeois ideologemes with which to fabricate its opposition,
than to re-activate indigenous bourgeois perspectives or to feed
off ideological 'seepage' from the West. In the event it is likely to
utilise the resources of all three. The evidence of the texts discussed here suggests that this is the case with Solzhenitsyn. His
proposals for the state are a case in point. Founded on a basic
authoritarianism which is retrieved from the Tsarist, feudal
past and reinforced by the invocation of Christian Orthodoxy,
the classically *liberal* separation of legislature, judiciary and
executive is introduced also. The transformation in
Solzhenitsyn's work of 'ethical socialism' into dictatorial moralism, of populism into elitism, investigation into prophecy,
and so on, is a process of considerable intricacy, drawing its
programmatic and affective inspiration from a wide range of
lineages to form an ideological structure which must be understood in its internal specificity, as well as in the ultimate implications which no doubt place it, in the last analysis, 'on the side
of' the bourgeoisie.

TECHNOCRAT AND PEASANTRY

The mediation in Solzhenitsyn's fiction of the developed ideology, that is to say its *aesthetic effect*, is to be discovered in *August 1914* which is, to date, the major novel of the post-1967 period.[39] It deals with the disastrous campaign against Germany of the Russian Second Army under General Samsonov in the first days of the 1914–18 war. A panoramic account of the advance, engagement and eventual destruction of the army provides the substance of the work, but of overriding importance for the present argument are the formal developments and ideological reorganisation that the text inaugurates over the previous fiction. Superficially *August 1914* resembles formally the earlier polyphonic novels: a range of ideologically distinct characters are juxtaposed to each other, becoming in turn the objects and bearers of a narrative that is not so much linear as accumulative. But in the book tendencies which earlier had been latent but constrained are exaggerated to the point where form itself is threatened. The foregrounding of a particular—ideologically numinous—character, Colonel Vorotyntsev, overreaches the 'democratic' balance between polyphony and centralisation of, say, *The First Circle*, and the result is the destruction of that kind of realist novel. The textual indices of this disruption are the introduction into the writing of the 'screen' passages of pseudo film script, of the historical documents and military communiqués, and of the extracts from contemporary newspapers that punctuate the fictional text with another kind of 'factual' discourse. Reaching towards the quasi-historiographical techniques of *The Gulag Archipelago*, these interpellations represent the impossibility of Solzhenitsyn sustaining the new ideological project within the fictional form previously available to him. Investing its ideological substantive almost solely in a central figure—Vorotyntsev—the totalising scope previously achieved by polyphony must now be compensated by pretence of strict historical veracity. Fictional writing, dominated by an explicit ideological falsehood, as will be argued, betrays itself in its own disintegration, necessitating a rearguard appeal to other forms of writing for external validation.

The general contour of the ideological emphases of *August*

1914 may be described in the first instance as the concatenation of a technocratic elitism with a peasant-based organicist irrationalism, a polarity evident in the political texts discussed above, and in fact constitutive, as will be subsequently shown, of *The Gulag Archipelago*. These preoccupations can be exposed in three main areas of the text: in Vorotyntsev, in that character's relationship with the peasant soldiers, and in the two accounts of the nature of historical development given by Varsonofiev, the scholar, and the engineer Obodovsky. Vorotyntsev stands out from the text as a prioritised figure. While *formally* he appears to take an egalitarian place among other characters as Nerzhin does among the prisoners at Mavrino, *ideologically* he is in the foreground to the extent that he dominates the book. Vorotyntsev is a close approximation to a 'positive hero'. The terms of this foregrounding consist essentially of an individualism which now achieves an uneasy, and at times impossible, coexistence with more organic, amorphous accounts of social activity. The contradictory unity of the earlier fiction now separates into mere opposition; two ideologies of Russian history, one bourgeois, the other nostalgically quasi-feudal, concatenate in an unresolved play of false solutions.

Vorotyntsev's setting, his necessary background, is the book's presentation of the other senior officers in the Russian army. Unlike the German high command, the Russian general staff is shown as a hidebound clique of time-servers. Promotion by seniority or favour advances the relentlessly mediocre and stifles the officers with initiative. The picture of seldom less than complacent inefficiency, counterpointed by the modern expertise of the German army, reaches claustrophobic maturity in Samsonov. 'Ponderous, baffled',[40] distracted by his quarrel with his superior Zhilinsky ('the living corpse'), unfitted by background or training for this command, the well-meaning but plodding general moves through the book from puzzled inability, through incomprehension and failing grasp, to an unhinged religious hysteria and despairing suicide. His own disintegration parallels that of his army. Mobilised too hastily, ill-equipped, detrained too early and forced to march without proper food or rest in the wrong direction, the advance of the Second Army degenerates from an optimistic crusade into a chaotic rout. Encircled and defeated, its generals in flight, all that remains to the soldiers is death or capture and isolated acts of individual endurance or bravery.

Yet within this narrative of uncontrollable misadventure, Vorotyntsev has a privileged mobility. He is detached from General Headquarters on a roving commission, and moves from section to section of the front attempting to modify the stupidity of his superiors. Here taking local command, there making discrete, friendly or manipulative suggestions, he tries to alter the direction of the campaign at both the strategic and the tactical levels. By inspired misinterpretation, or sometimes open disobedience of orders Vorotyntsev attempts to impose his own vision on the army, not usually by authority but by intervention and *management*. His role is negative in the sense that in the situation all he is capable of doing is partially to repair the damage done by the commanding officers, but positive in the ideological values his action embodies. Against the ostentatious traditionalism of the Russian command, Vorotyntsev is a modernist; a military professional of a new kind. A graduate of the General Staff Academy, he belongs to a semi-notorious generation of junior officers from the class of Professor Golovin who have since come to be known as the 'Young Turks'. These officers 'and perhaps a handful of engineers as well' knew that 'what Russia needed was modern technology, modern organisation and alert, active minds'. While the rest of the Russian army, and the rest of Russia, is locked in what are, for the Young Turks, the outmoded struggles of the nineteenth century, they are entering a 'new era'.[41] They study modern military strategy, read army textbooks by German generals, and prepare themselves for a war whose outcome cannot any longer depend upon 'common patriotism' but on efficiency and technique. They, and Vorotyntsev prominent among them, are military technocrats. The colonel's personal qualities are somewhat too happily matched to this ideological role;

straight-backed and alert, he has a direct, frank gaze; his mind is sharp and quick, his manner decisive and energetic. Neither arrogant nor submissive, he calmly assesses each situation and acts. Dynamic where his superiors are pedestrian, tireless and precise where they are lazy, the idealised Vorotyntsev moves in a clear direction: 'The obsession which throbbed within him was to solve a *riddle*; his destiny was to take a *decision* . . .'[42]

Vorotyntsev's narrative and ideological role is highlighted by the action around the village of Usdau.[43] This is the critical battle of the campaign and failure here threatens the security of the army headquarters and would open the way to the German destruction of the entire Russian force in East Prussia. The action is bungled by the Russian general in local command, but Vorotyntsev, on his own initiative, takes over the organisation of a semi-spontaneous counter-attack that partially retrieves the situation for the Second Army. While ultimately not even Solzhenitsyn's Vorotyntsev can fly entirely in the face of history and turn the tide of the overall campaign, the implication of his placement at this crucial juncture, and of the freelance nature of his intervention outside the official command structure, is ideologically redolent. Behind Vorotyntsev lies an ideology of expertise. The assumption that feeds this character's deployment is that of the possibility of social or historical processes being centred or ordered by the transcendent individual. Where in *The First Circle* potentially centralising characters are held in balance by a *decentred* text, in *August 1914* Vorotyntsev supervenes in a *fragmenting* text, fragmenting at the levels of subject matter, narrative form, and (in the intrusion of the 'non-fictional' discourses) of writing itself. Such an individualistic assumption is dangerous, shading easily into the political and moral elitism witnessed by Solzhenitsyn's non-fictional writing of this period.

Over against this gifted individual, and the ideological imperative he bears, are the peasant masses that constitute the conscript army. In writing them Solzhenitsyn appeals to quite different ideological and affective resources from those mobilised in Vorotyntsev; rather than technocratic, modernistic individualism, the peasantry are drawn straight from the countryside of a mystified rural Russia of the nineteenth century. For them there is not Vorotyntsev's decisiveness, but passive suffering and endurance. The peasantry is indeed, for Solzhenitsyn, a mass: not the active classes of real history, but an ideologically processed amorphousness—Nerzhin's 'People' put into uniform. Largely undifferentiated, either individually or sociologically, the peasantry is subordinated to a unitary portrayal that constructs in the Russian countryside the essence of the 'national character'—that familiar conservative myth—and dissolves their historical specificity into a sentimental image of childlike simplicity. In a single self-conscious authorial intervention in the book, in the first part of Chapter 40, Solzhenitsyn speaks directly of the peasants in nostalgic contradistinction to the 'degeneration' of the Russian people in the post-revolutionary period. He regrets that there are no photographs of these men because 'since then our national make-up has changed completely . . . and no camera-lens can ever again find those trusting, bearded men, those friendly eyes, those placid, selfless faces'![44] The patronage of these images is blatant, and is repeated in the role given the peasant soldiers by the narrative. The major sections of the book in which rank and file soldiers are identifiably present are those passages dealing with the battle at Usdau (where, significantly, Vorotyntsev is also most clearly drawn). Here, under shellfire which factitiously reinforces the ideological colouring, the peasant soldiers are reduced to a static material. Sheltering in the trenches under a ferocious German bombardment, they have no idea of flight, of course, (unlike the revolutionary Lenartovich), but display a dull-witted endurance of the gunfire: 'Ingrained in them was the lesson inherited from their forefathers, the inexorable lesson of centuries: suffering must be borne; there is no way out.'[45] This passivity is not merely the effect of the battle but is constitutive of Solzhenitsyn's approbatory portrayal of the peasantry. His peasant soldiers with their 'innocence' and their 'great-hearted smiles' are the creatures of a reactionary myth of the naive but morally exalted countryside.

Juxtaposition of Vorotyntsev and the peasantry reveals the ideological problematic of *August 1914*. Activist individualism and a passive people dominated by inexorable suffering are but two sides of the same ideological coin. The peasantry, good but simple, are material of Vorotyntsev's organising role. His dynamism can only be realised if it can be counterpointed by, and exercised upon, a willing but unmotivated mass; the elitist needs the enduring people from whom he is thus differentiated. And for their part the peasantry, leaderless from within, and lacking the energy or independence of mind to act for themselves, are there to be managed by the technocrat while enshrining within themselves the sources of the national strength. There is nothing here of the open, exploratory structures of the earlier fiction, but rather a closed series of polarities that mystify and mythologise class and history.

The same polarity as the Vorotyntsev-peasantry couple, with slightly altered terms, is to be found in the two commentators on history, Obodovsky and Varsonofiev, whose—mutually irreconcilable—viewpoints orbit the central passages of the text in silent complicity. Obodovsky is the 'Vorotyntsev' of this polarity. A 'bourgeois specialist', he has abandoned his political past as an anarchist revolutionary for which he twice suffered imprisonment and exile, and has returned to Russia as a brilliant, if peripatetic, engineer. He is the author of textbooks on economics and the layout of ports, and other trade and industrial subjects, as well as specialised works on mining. He appears in the book in the course of a tour of the centres of Russian engineering industry. Like Vorotyntsev he has a surplus of energy. His general dynamism—described by himself as an always imminent explosion, as if he were a samovar about to burst with the pressure of steam within—is supplemented by his careless dress and violent, uncoordinated gestures to give an aura of careering activism, a terrible personal ferment. He sleeps for four hours in every twenty-four and talks incessantly. He desires, again like Vorotyntsev, to shape the history of Russia with his own hands. The engineers of the early part of the century are to play an important ideological role in *The Gulag Archipelago* where they become the *type* of Solzhenitsyn's appeal to a putative past technocracy, and in *August 1914* Obodovsky, one of that 'handful of engineers' allied with the Young Turks in their apprehension of a 'new era', plays a similar part.[46] With his idealised personal qualities, the 'frank' smile, for example, 'of a man with nothing to hide',[47] he is the object of powerful authorial endorsement. This is tellingly indicated by the fact that his views on Russian expansion in the North-East are word for word those of Solzhenitsyn himself in the *Letter to Soviet Leaders*.[48]

The political affiliations, the anti-democratic orientation, of Obodovsky's dynamic technical specialism, are revealed in his discussion with the young revolutionaries Naum and Sonya.[49] Against demands for social revolution—lopsidedly portrayed as a naive emotionalism—Obodovsky calls for unimpeded industrial development, and wilfully dismisses consideration of the political forms this might take. He rejects governmental power as a 'dead horse' and suggests instead that a technocratic layer of engineers and technicians should exercise less obvious but more powerful direction of the country through the deployment of resources and expertise. For him revolutionaries are destroyers, and morally despicable beside engineers whom he characterises as builders. The question of whether this rapid industrialisation should be the development of a *capitalist* industry he dismisses with irritated haste. When Naum maintains that unless industrial development is organised in a new way it will lead to nothing but increased exploitation of the people, Obodovsky produces the familiar and lame dicta that such a question could only be asked by immature arts students who fail to understand that the technocrats and administrators make the major contribution to industrial production, and, if anyone, it is they, the middle class specialists, who are exploited. The argument is as superficial as it is misconceived. But Obodovsky's position is *portrayed* in these passages as the stronger one because his political opponents are never allowed by Solzhenitsyn to do more than sneer and utter slogans. The apparent debate between them is in fact no more than a vehicle for Obodovsky's rejection of political democracy and economic reorganisation, in favour of a middle class technocratic solution. Whereas in the forms of the earlier fiction this could have been a genuine exchange, here the result is ever pre-given, questioned only to be confirmed, monistic rather than dialectical.

Simple technocratic ideology is not, however, enough. The new demands of Solzhenitsyn's project also call for a 'spiritual' element in the system, an irrationalism which can allow the ineffable back into the apparently confident, managerial rationalism of Obodovsky's perspective. This is supplied by his other side, his ghostly double in the text, Varsonofiev, who takes the place in *this* polarity of Solzhenitsyn's nostalgic peasantry. He is the scholarly spokesman of an organic irrationalism, seemingly at odds with, but actually complementary to, Obodovsky's position.

From the first Varsonofiev is an enigma. His presence is mediated through the two students Kotya and Sanya who see him at work in the library and speculate about the nature of his research which is left unspecified throughout: they name him 'the Stargazer'. It is not until their last night in Moscow before volunteering for service in the army that the boys make contact with the scholar, who takes them to a beer hall and discusses their philosophies. Kotya is an Hegelian and Sanya a Tolstoyan. Varsonofiev's questions and replies are cryptic and elusive. He exposes contradictions in the positions of the two students—between, for example, Tolstoyan pacifism and 'patriotic' duty to the state—but his own views are veiled and obscure. He tells riddles and answers questions with questions. Against the boys' search for answers Varsonofiev emphasises the difficulties of the questions, against their programmatic clarity, he admires eclecticism and mystery: 'When things are too clear they are no longer interesting.'[50] There is in Varsonofiev a wilful puzzlement, quietly provocative, which deliberately fends off the kind of thinking that could lead to constructive action. Towards the end of the passage however, Kotya and Sanya do force the elderly scholar to some positive statements. He is, not surprisingly, no admirer of democracy, and ridicules any attempt to speak of 'the people' or the 'intelligentsia', not simply because he dislikes categorisation as a habit of mind, but thinks 'scientific' thinking an impossibility. His attitude to the students' idealism—again naively portrayed—is cynical and petulant. Politics, for Varsonofiev, is a kind of conceit that seeks to devise ideal institutions, whereas the correct position is to stand back and develop the personal soul. Indeed society is not capable of *development*; in Varsonofiev's view, this word can only apply to the spiritual qualities of the individual consciousness. And this development, in a significant term, is one of *'divination'*: there is, for example, 'a justice which existed before us, without us and for its own sake'[51] and men must divine what it is. The rejection of politics for the spiritual interior is founded on Varsonofiev's overriding tenet that 'history is *irrational* . . . It has its own . . . organic structure.'[52] This organicism reminiscent of the organic pole of the ideology of *The Gulag Archipelago* is expressed in a paragraph of natural images: history is a tree which cannot be made to grow better by applying reason to it, or in an image for revolution, an axe; or it is a river whose flow cannot be blocked or interrupted. The simple technical inadequacy of the metaphors is symptomatic of the falsification behind them. As rivers can be diverted or blocked, and the growth of trees modified, there is a telling infelicity in the metaphoric reinforcement of the irrationalism that Varsonofiev articulates. And ultimately the enigmatic qualities of his discourse break down; despite his flaunted disdain for politics, or practical answers to theoretical questions, Varsonofiev is unambiguous in his support for the boys joining the army. Having said that it is impossible to judge right behaviour which depends upon the private convictions of the individual, Varsonofiev does not shrink from a 'feeling' that Russia's spiritual health depends upon young men going to war. The elaborate enigma of his views fails entirely to mask the reactionary character of the political position they supervene.

Soviet criticism has repeatedly remarked that the implicit suggestion of *August 1914* is that Russia should have taken 'another path'. This is undoubtedly a correct judgement of the book, and is evident from the anti-revolutionary, and even anti-political, character of the book's polar ideological structure; technocratic elitism and organicist irrationalism. It is explicit in the character Lenartovich, the strongest spokesman in the book of the revolutionary outlook. Fiercely intelligent, but over-confident, the young middle-class politician, conscripted into the army against his will, is drawn as a caricature. His revolutionary politics are presented in the course of the degeneration of the military campaign in East Prussia as no more than a selfish veneer which, as Lenartovich is exposed to greater degrees of personal danger, becomes no more than hollow rationalisation for cowardice and a lack of the kind of character strength displayed by Vorotyntsev and his stoical peasantry. Lenartovich eventually deserts his unit and attempts to surrender to the Germans; his own life and political work, he decides opportunistically, are more important than the safety of the private soldiers entrusted to him, or the success of the campaign. Significantly it is Vorotyntsev whom Lenartovich encounters when lost in the forest, who is to tell the scared and discredited revolutionary that at such a time of national crisis political differences no longer matter. With a bland moral universalism—as usual, for Solzhenitsyn, foregrounded and fundamental—the only difference that matters now is that between 'decency and swinishness'.[53]

This moralism is a signal retreat from real history—an history that *August 1914* as an 'historical novel' enticingly offers at the same time as it conceals. The ethical-ideological substantive is not negotiated as a practical political activity within society, but is counterposed to society as a transcendent. Such an operation must necessarily enforce a distortion of the social picture of the book in order to re-encompass its own flouting of the historically real. This is undertaken by the selectivity of the class relationships of the book—dominantly those between Vorotyntsev and the peasantry. The partiality of such a portrayal, which places with imaginary centrality an eccentric class relationship at the heart of a text purporting to realism, can only be taken, not as realism, but as optative, articulating by selectivity Solzhenitsyn's version of society, emphasising the only elements of history that he is prepared to admit to full validity. The pieces missing from the picture are as significant as its presences. As usual, the urban proletariat is omitted, nor is there a proletarian or even peasant spokesman for a political vision. The peasantry itself is locked within a literary idealisation, and the other classes of Russian society are by and large written out of history. This kind of concealment by portrayal is only a special case of the operation conducted by the ideological structure of the book in any case, and has the same explanation. It is not that Vorotyntsev or some of his views are necessarily odious—energy and expertise may well be admirable in certain circumstances; nor is it simply that Solzhenitsyn's version of some of the qualities of the Russian peasantry is entirely false. It is the *structure* of these portrayals, their inclusiveness and exclusiveness, and their relationship to real history, (the ideological implication of the emphasis of the structure) that carry out a mystificatory function. They strive, and succeed, in making it impossible for certain *questions* (such as that of revolution, the genuinely central historical issue) to be raised in the book in any other than an already-answered form.

Ideology is never simply true or false. It is given rise to by objective social forces and bears a real determinate relationship to a reality that lies beyond itself and to which it can only obliquely refer. But what it must do is to suppress any understanding of the method of its production. This is so with the dual ideological structure of *August 1914*. By absorbing all of history into a false play of rationalism and irrationalism, technocracy and organicist nostalgia, while simultaneously prioritising these as 'the historical', the book necessarily suppresses any account of the mechanisms which bring such an orientation to history into being. It is in the questions that cannot be asked or answered, in the opacity of ideology, that its mystificatory function lies, and not in any deficiency of the book's internal 'truth'. Within the book's own terms Vorotyntsev and Obodovsky are indeed admirable, the peasantry are indeed engagingly childlike, and the revolutionaries morally despicable. It could not have been any other way, because the system of questions and answers in which the book's ideological structure consists determine this from the start.

But the problem that is raised for criticism, although not for *August 1914* itself, for the text's own 'answers' to its putative 'questions' about the nature of society and of history are inevitably 'satisfactory', is that of the historical status of the book. *August 1914* is not a novel 'about' the first month of the 1914–18 war, but refers, rather, to contemporary Soviet society. It is a system of implicit proposals and criticisms of *post*-revolutionary Russian history written back into a numinous pseudo-past. This system derives from and is determined by the (anti-Marxist) project of Solzhenitsyn's non-fictional writing of the period, and thus moulds the fictional in order to equate it to certain pre-given, non-aesthetic dictates. Set within a fundamentally moral and not historical framework, the book cannot thus admit fully historical questions and answers, but is instead in an only imaginary relationship with its ostensible historical subject matter. But it has a directly effective relationship with its contemporary time to which it offers moral exhortations, political proposal and suasive affective images. *August 1914* is not concerned with the discovery and depiction of an historical situation, but with giving fictional fabric to an ideological structure that pre-exists it. This is not so with the early fiction. There the ideological framework provides a *field* within which discovery and development, contradiction and irresolution may be admitted, an 'unfinished', complex exploration. But in *August 1914* there is no critical distance between the ideological project and the fictional representations, but the one enslaves the other, shaping its images for no other purpose than its own validification.

Solzhenitsyn's fictional reconstruction of history in *August 1914* must stand or fall together with the explicit politics of the other documents of the period, for their 'solutions' are identical. The attitude of the present argument to those politics has been made sufficiently clear already, but its criticism must be extended to an equally abrasive aesthetic evaluation of *August 1914*. Nostalgia in fiction or in political theorising can never be acceptable and is certainly valueless (although not without a real effectivity) when it constitutes itself together with a reactionary elitism as a seemingly genuine attempt to understand and, by implication, alter the history of a country whose past has already been mystified enough and can only be vitiated by further distortion. The coyly robust idealising of the novel's 'positive' characters, the selectivity of its social and historical picture, the closure of its ideological structure and the reactionary character of its evident, authorially endorsed conceptual content makes *August 1914* a text of considerable ideological interest, but meagre artistic value. Just as the ideological and the fictional are coterminous in this book, so the political and aesthetic judgements of it must coincide.

MACHINE, ORGANISM, SOUL

In charting the artistic and ideological development of Solzhenitsyn's writing the two texts which may be taken as datum points of particular importance are *One Day in the Life of Ivan Denisovich* and *The Gulag Archipelago*.[54] In the case of *Ivan Denisovich* there was proposed above an interpretative model which saw the book's empirical and 'valueless' character as having twofold importance: it represented a break with previous official 'illustrating literature' and simultaneously reflected central characteristics of Soviet society atomised and depoliticised by the rule of the Stalinist bureaucracy. This duality was a threshold which could have paved the way for a new and radical, analytic Soviet literature, and yet could also remain tied to an empirical and static reportage of phenomena subsumed under a structure constituted of abstract, superhistorical and in the end desperately reactionary values. It is this latter possibility, the rehearsal of the terrible facts of Soviet history organised in the service of a retrogressive ideology, that is realised in *The Gulag Archipelago*.

The book appears to be a *history* of the repressive apparatus and of 'that amazing country' of Gulag, but most editions of it (although not the English language version) are subtitled 'An experiment in artistic investigation', which has a quite different epistemological status, less authoritative than that of a 'history'. The book extensively and repetitively catalogues the entire repertoire of the Stalinist atrocities from the moment of arbitrary arrest, through the process of interrogation, mental and physical torture, to trial or extra-judicial sentencing; it recounts the intermediate stays in the transit prisons, the MVD internal prisons and the 'boxes' in which prisoners *en route* were kept at railway stations. Solzhenitsyn writes of the journeys made by prisoners in the red cattle trucks in which entire nations were deported, in the ships and barges across the White Sea to the notorious Solovetsky Islands camps, and in the prison vans variously camouflaged from the rest of the population with the brightly-painted labels MEAT, BREAD or DRINK SOVIET CHAMPAGNE. The account arrives finally at the labour camps, sometimes no more than a sign nailed to a fir tree where the prisoners had first to erect the barbed wire and watchtowers that contained them.

Solzhenitsyn records the many 'waves' of mass arrests and deportations that punctuated the Stalinist period and shows that there were many more of them than the officially acknowledged 'excesses' of 1936–8. He details the political articles of the Soviet penal code, their subsections and the various 'dialectical' extensions which transformed them from instruments of Soviet law into the formal rationale for repression: Solzhenitsyn himself was arrested under article 58–11 which provides for anti-Soviet organisation—the 'organisation' in this case consisting of Solzhenitsyn and the friend to whom he wrote letters critical of Stalin. He writes poignantly on one of his favourite themes of Gulag as a secret country within, but distant from, the rest of society, whose natives are like a strange, foreign people. And with psychological acuteness he portrays the officials of the 'security' services whose motivations and conscious desires he exposes in a series of vignettes, caricatures and anecdotes. In the second volume Solzhenitsyn describes the growth of the Archipelago through successive 'metastases' from the first institutions on the Solovetsky Islands into a nationwide network of labour camps and political prisons.

There is much in *The Gulag Archipelago* that is new. Roy Medvedev, the dissident Russian historian, who writes from a position critical of Solzhenitsyn and from prolonged study of Stalinism, remarks that 'Soviet readers—even those who well remember the 20th and 22nd Congresses of the Party—know hardly one tenth of the facts recounted by Solzhenitsyn: Our youth, indeed, does not know even a one hundredth of them.'[55] Some of Solzhenitsyn's facts are wrong. Medvedev points out a number of errors— the deportations from Leningrad in 1934–5 after the murder of Kirov were numbered in tens of thousands and not the half-million that Solzhenitsyn proposes; similarly the number of peasants arrested during the forced collectivisation is exaggerated; and after Stalin's death it was not ten officials of the MVD-MGB who were imprisoned or shot but nearer a hundred (although this is still a minute figure compared with the many criminals who retained positions of power and prestige in the state bureaucracy or, like Molotov, enjoyed a comfortable retirement). But it is not the facts that Solzhenitsyn brings to light that reveal the writer, for this information—if it were ever widely disseminated in the Soviet Union—could only speed the rebirth of political opposition among the mass of the people and aid the completion of the 'unfinished revolution'. In order to understand Solzhenitsyn and his importance for the development of Soviet society it is necessary to dissect not only what he tells us but also how and why he does so, to separate the content from the form. To exchange 'facts' with Solzhenitsyn, welcome his revelations and regret his ideological backwardness is, at this stage in his career, after exile to the West, both politically inadequate and critically superficial. To do this is to fall into the trap of 'moralistic politics' as Ernest Mandel, faltering on the edge of it himself, characterises the problematic of *The Gulag Archipelago*.[56] It is of course true, as Medvedev says, that Solzhenitsyn's account is 'one-sided'—from an examination of one aspect of Soviet history he draws conclusions designed to describe its totality, and it is equally the case that his version of what he does undertake to describe is often partial and distorted—his treatment, for example, of the foreign intervention and White Terror which provoked Bolshevik retaliation is cursory—but the shape and intentions of *The Gulag Archipelago* are determined by forces which have their roots deep in Soviet society, and to chide Solzhenitsyn in hurt tones for not having told a truth that resides outside the ideological area that his work defines is to succumb to an emotional liberalism that abdicates from the task of explanation that must precede and condition judgement.

To go deeply into that collective history of which *The Gulag Archipelago* is a refracted product is beyond the scope of this study, but even a schematic account of the nature of the Soviet intelligentsia will gather important clues to an understanding of Solzhenitsyn's work. The ideology of *The Gulag Archipelago* is composed of two main structural elements: these have been termed here the 'technocratic' and the 'organic', and each is based in a different phase of the history of the intelligentsia—the former representing the current material relationships of this group 'in ideal form', and the latter a conservative retrieval of older values.

The contemporary intelligentsia is dominated by its technical and scientific layer. This domination dates from the early thirties when the persecution of the old technical intelligentsia—amongst whom the engineers, singled out as scapegoats for certain weaknesses of the economy and branded 'wreckers', received special attention—was reversed. As Mary McAuley points out,[57] initially necessary and temporary measures hardened under Stalin into economic principles, two of which were the emphases—largely unchanged to the present day—on the expansion of heavy industry and the production of arms. To facilitate this development a layer of scientific and technical experts was needed, prompting Stalin to decree in 1931 in the fifth of his 'Six Conditions' for construction: 'We must move from a policy of destruction of the old technical in-telligentsia to a policy of concern for it, of making use of it.'[58] From this point stems the modern intelligentsia, playing a paramount part both in the real economy and in official ideo-logy. This intelligentsia has increasingly overlapped with sec-tions of the ruling elite, participating in the running of state political, economic and police institutions. The subjective de-mands of this group are various: Ticktin argues that there can be few members of the ruling group, apart from professional policemen and the utterly cynical, who do not share to some de-gree the desires of the intelligentsia for democratisation.[59] Wider discussion on, for example, economic issues, articulated by the *dissident* intelligentsia as a political principle, would be a way for the incorporated intelligentsia to enhance their own position and also to find solutions to the pressing problems in this field at a time of increasing awareness of the failure of traditional dogmatism. Those members of the lower intelligentsia, not directly part of the ruling group, although aspiring to its privileges, are restrained from open dissent by their dependence on that group for employment and wait for a cue from above. And those within the governing group fear that 'liberalisation' for the intellectuals might lead to political opposition among the working classes which would fundamentally challenge their position as an elite. Instead 'private' freedoms are instituted: prohibited books circulate freely among the elite and otherwise banned films may be seen at special cinemas. This is underpinned by the envelope system of unofficial payments that sup-plement official salaries. The objective, material interests of the intelligentsia *as a group* are tied to those of the ruling stratum and support individualistic ideologies of self-advancement.

The political positions taken up by the dissident intelligentsia vary widely but centre on the advocacy of technocratic and frequently pro-capitalist reforms, often coupled, as in Sakharov's early statements, with a compassion for 'the common man'. The technocratic ideology in Solzhenitsyn's work derives from this intelligentsia of which he is a part and is homologous with the material relations of this group with the rest of society and with the ruling group; these relations lend themselves, particularly in the present conjuncture of emerging 'managerial' solutions, to the advocacy of technocratic leadership which feeds on the depoliticisation of society that Stalinism has already effected.

The organic, 'peasant', element of Solzhenitsyn's ideology represents an historical nostalgia for a lost wholeness, a reaction from the atomisation of Soviet society which seeks in an ideal, undifferentiated peasantry imbued with a stylised moral simplicity an alternative to the spiritual vacuum of bureaucratic rule. This ideology bases itself on the peasant-orientated intelligentsia of the revolutionary and immediately post-revolutionary period. During the revolution the intelligentsia fragmented. The forces of liberal democracy who had, with the socialists, opposed Tsarism were divided by October when the constitutional reforms based on a desired form of bourgeois parliamentarianism were outstripped by the socialist measures of the Bolsheviks supported by the mass of the people. Trotsky, writing in 1924, describes the variety of currents that existed within even the literary intelligentsia, basically sympathetic to the revolution, and also points the peasant connection:

The non-communist intelligentsia which has not thrown in its lot unreservedly with the proletariat, and this comprises the overwhelming majority of the intelligentsia, seeks support in the peasantry because of the absence, or rather, the extreme weakness of bourgeois support. For the time being, this process has a purely preparatory and symbolic character, and expresses itself (with hindsight) in the idealization of the peasant elements of the Revolution. This peculiar neo-

populism is characteristic of all the fellow-travelers. Later
on, with the growth of the number of schools in the villages
and of those who can read, the bond between this art and the
peasantry may become more organic. At the same time, the
peasantry will develop a creative intelligentsia of its own.
The peasant point of view, in politics, and in art, is more primitive, more limited, more egotistic, than that of the proletariat. But this peasant point of view exists and will continue to
exist for a long time and very earnestly.[60]

To this must be added the various elements of the intelligentsia
who either sided with the White forces in the name of a return to
Tsarism or continued to agitate for an intermediate bourgeois
period. These groups largely lost their basis during the Civil
War and their members were either killed, imprisoned or exiled
forming the basis of the White emigré tradition which Solzhenitsyn, for all the liberal populism of this zone of his ideology, can
at times invoke as an alternative to Stalinism.[61]

The intelligentsia of the twenties, then, contained many sub-
scribers to an ideology of 'peasant liberalism' derived from the
populist agitation of the preceding century which had varied in
form from the anarchism of Narodnaya Volya, steeped in a
mystic self-immersion in an idea of the peasantry, to the more
collectivist revolutionary positions of the Social Revolutionaries who, contemporary with the Bolsheviks, were also
peasant-orientated. Solzhenitsyn invests in the peasantry a
long-suffering endurance (an oblique function of his own authoritarianism) and the nostalgically simple morality of old Holy
Russia 'when the distinction between good and evil was very
simply perceived by the heart'.[62] Upon the basis of this idea are
founded Solzhenitsyn's explicitly religious positions which
range from high moral didacticism to a mystic inwardness. And
his peasantry is supplemented by his idea of the political prisoners as a nation, the inhabitants of the 'country' of Gulag:
Nerzhin, in *The First Circle*, has already articulated a populism
in which the place of 'the People' is taken by the prison population.

The early years of the revolution were a period of considerable freedom and creativity for the intelligentsia, and also saw the emergence and consolidation of a scientific and technical layer. The engineers and other technical experts based in the expansion of Russian industry in the pre-revolutionary period had opposed Tsarism as an hindrance to the development of the productive forces and had, more or less grudgingly, acquiesced in the revolution as technologically and economically progressive. It is to this group that Solzhenitsyn turns for one of the rare, imagined, fusions of the two poles of his own ideology. The following portrayal of the engineers of the twenties seeks to combine the spiritualising idealism of the peasant-orientated, non-Marxist intelligentsia with the technologistic modernism of the technical layers:

> I could remember the engineers of the twenties very well indeed: their open, shining intellects, their free and gentle humor, their agility and breadth of thought, the ease with which they shifted from one engineering field to another, and . . . from technology to social concerns and art. Then, too, they personified good manners and delicacy of taste; well-bred speech that flowed evenly and was free of uncultured words; one of them might play a musical instrument, another dabble in painting; and their faces always bore a spiritual imprint.[63]

This image, which reads like one of Trotsky's more lyrical visions of future, Communist, man, is Solzhenitsyn's remembered and proposed technocratic elite.

To identify these two determinate *poles* of Solzhenitsyn's ideology is to run the risk of essentialising his work, of identifying an essence of which everything else is merely epiphenomenal. It must be acknowledged that *The Gulag Archipelago*, while representing in the most developed and extreme form this dual ideological structure (which was latent in the earlier work but crystallises here) has an immediate complexity which appears at times as personal confusion on the author's part.

Admiring evocations of the society of Holy Russia jostle with
liberal-democratic proposals, universal human compassion
with extreme Russian chauvinism. All should be given their
due within the basic ideological structure which is *disrupted* by
these contradictory positions rather than reflected in them.
This complexity derives in part from the fact that *The Gulag
Archipelago* is an archaeology of the author's previous positions,
which are not necessarily identical with the ideological parameters of the book itself. Indeed, within Solzhenitsyn's work as
a whole there is a chronological shift between the two main
elements: while both are present in *The Gulag Archipelago,*
Solzhenitsyn's populism tends to predominate in the earlier
work and the technocratic elitism emerges during the development of his writing, reaching clarity here. And the organic element itself undergoes internal mutation, the later religiosity
displacing the previous 'peasantism'.

This bifurcated ideology can be seen at work most clearly in
Solzhenitsyn's understanding of history, but this must first be
situated within the epistemology and the methodology of the
book. Solzhenitsyn announces in the Dedication the partial
nature of his account of Soviet history. He gives the book to
those who did not survive the camps and asks to be forgiven for
not having seen or remembered, 'for not having divined it all'.
His relationship to the object of artistic investigation is one of
memory and divination—a curiously, but appropriately,
arcane expression—and this double process of, on the one
hand, seeing, the sensuous apprehension of phenomena, and
memory, the personal retention of sensuous fact, and on the
other a mysterious reading of facts, is a version of
Solzhenitsyn's general epistemology. It mixes a quasi-scientific
regard for sources, information, itemisation, with the organic
irrationality by which Solzhenitsyn leaps from collected facts to
historical generalisation. He sees himself not as one who has a
knowledge of history, but as one who has *experienced* it, and must
speak out. From the start the project is one of exposure which is,
to the extent that what is concealed is not the whole, a project of
distortion. Not only intention but also opportunity conspire in

this partiality: when introducing a chronological list of 'waves' of mass arrests, Solzhenitsyn regrets its incompleteness, 'limited by my own capacity to penetrate the past'.[64] 'Penetrate', as 'divined', suggests a privileged, esoteric relationship with history. Side by side, however, with intuitive perception is a painstaking empiricism; Solzhenitsyn carefully thanks the 227 'witnesses' who supplied him with reports and letters, and the researchers who found 'supporting bibliographical material'.

Within personal relationships also Solzhenitsyn vaunts an irrational epistemology. Writing of a prisoner he encountered, Georgi Kramarenko, he remembers that he made up his mind about this man before he had had time to 'think things over'. Instead 'a spiritual relay, a sensor relay, had clicked' inside the writer and closed him off from Kramarenko for ever. In a strange mixture of the technological and the intuitive this inner sense, both 'spiritual' and 'secret', 'a constant, inborn trait', yet also a 'sensor relay', provides instant, automatic judgements before, and without, analytic thought.[65] But the relationship between the intuitive and the empirical remains enigmatic; Solzhenitsyn offers no link between them and so the foundations of his judgements are left unclear. Was, for example, Solzhenitsyn's belief that 'Russia . . . was obviously not suited for any sort of socialism whatsoever' gathered from letters and memoirs or was it an intuitive leap? The reader is suspicious because he knows that Solzhenitsyn will *guess* when he does not know: seeking to expose Bolshevik atrocities he remarks that 'knowing the *sense and spirit* of the Revolution, it is easy to guess' that the prisons were filled even as early as October and November 1917.[66] Unable to produce even many facts of *Bolshevik* repression, particularly not during the first months of the revolution before the intervention and the White Terror, Solzhenitsyn has to guess, or perhaps rely on his 'spiritual relay'. And although Solzhenitsyn's epistemological method is an unreconciled concatenation of bare fact and supposition, he frequently shows but little regard even for the empirical bases of his judgements: he more than once sets aside the many 'tiny

ups and downs' of a particular subject which would only interest 'a historian pursuing *all the details* of those years'.[67]

On a scale larger than that of particular statement, the general polarity of the epistemology is repeated in the form of the
book which is predominantly anecdotal. The anecdote, usually
vivid, sometimes distractingly humorous and always moving, is
the basic unit of Solzhenitsyn's narrative and is given a precise
function: it forms the basis, and helps to obscure the assertive
status, of general observations on Soviet history. Solzhenitsyn's
account of the process of arrest illustrates his general method.
An initial statement—that there were many different kinds of
arrest—is followed by a series of anecdotes including an ironic
compliment to the secret police for their virtuosity at a time
when other cultural forms seemed to evince the uniformity of
mass-production: and this preludes a generalised 'historical'
statement—'political arrests were distinguished . . . by the fact
that people were arrested who were guilty of nothing'.[68] The
progression is from uncontentious statement, through diverting
anecdote, to historical conclusions which are far from the realm
of absolute truth that Solzhenitsyn insists other men should
inhabit. It is true that many were arrested who were guilty of
nothing but this is far from saying that this was the defining
characteristic of all political arrests, and it is far from the last
word on Soviet society. Solzhenitsyn indulges in silent exagger-
ation under the cover of anecdotal 'evidence'.

Similarly deceptive is the repetitiveness of the catalogue of
crimes. The events which form the basis for Solzhenitsyn's
chapter on the chronology of repression are also cited when he
itemises the articles of the penal code. He even seems to flinch
as if overwhelmed by a mass of information, and then, acknow-
ledging the recurrence of material he has already used, he warns
the reader that he may bore him with repetition and then
repeats nonetheless.[69] The impression is conveyed of more material than is actually presented.

If the two elements of the technocratic and organic exist in
the epistemology and form of the book (empirical data/
intuitive, 'spiritual' divination; factual anecdote/historical

generalisation) this is no less true of the wider categorial resources of *The Gulag Archipelago*. The very process of history is
imagined by Solzhenitsyn within these ideological poles. His
idea of history resides in two major groups of organising
images: technological images which figure history as a process
imaginable in terms of machine-like mechanisms which may be
understood to have certain definable structures and perhaps
even to operate in accordance with historical laws; and organic
images which feed a view of history as a natural process, given,
and detached from human volition or responsibility. The first
of these groups predominates in the book. The repressive
apparatus is described as 'Our Sewage Disposal system' and as
a 'meat grinder'; it is a 'Great Machine' whose 'Engine Room'
is the special courts where 'The machine stamped out the sentences'.[70] Solzhenitsyn speaks of the process of interrogation as
'the grinding of our souls in the gears of the great Nighttime Institution'.[71] Associated with these images are those which
record the dehumanisation of the people involved. The interrogator is 'an anonymous cog in the whole machine', the personnel of the *apparatus* do their work of imprisonment and
interrogation in accordance with 'schedules', and 'The real law
underlying the arrests . . . was *the assignment of quotas*, the
norms set, the planned allocations'.[72] The view which inheres
in these images is one which sees Stalinist repression as a vast
anonymous mechanism which processes prisoners like a
packing factory; but it is a machine without an operator; it
has lost any rationale that it might once have had: torture, for
example, was rarely used to elicit truth but was an automatic
part of 'an inevitably filthy procedure'.[73] This technological
imagery of the state as a machine supports the technocratic
ideology that it could best be run by engineers.

Side by side with the mechanical are Solzhenitsyn's organic
images of history. In a telling mixture of magic and nature he
refers to the prison camps, amplifying the natural image of
the book's title, as the 'spellbound archipelago'. The various
mass arrests he imagines as 'waves' which, combining with
technological imagery, rush through the pipes of the sewage

disposal system. Waves of sufficient dimension become rivers and the history of Stalinist repression is 'the history of an endless swallow and flow; flood alternating with ebb and ebb again with flood; waves pouring in, some big, some small; brooks and rivulets ... trickles ... and then just plain individually scooped-up droplets'.[74] The meaning of this natural imagery becomes clearer when Solzhenitsyn is describing one of the waves in which personnel of the apparatus themselves suffered: 'the State Security officers—who got caught in a *wave* were in very serious danger ... A wave is a natural catastrophe and even more powerful than the *Organs* themselves.'[75] A natural catastrophe: that is how Solzhenitsyn sees what is, for his technocratic ideology, the Great Machine. It is an elemental force stronger than the most powerful human institutions. The idea is reinforced by a cluster of supplementary images which stress the 'naturalness' of Stalinism: mass arrests were 'epidemics' and the repressive apparatus is imagined as a 'dragon', a 'monster', a 'tapeworm' and even as the circulatory system of the human body: if the political prisoners are the bloodstream, then the non-political offenders and the habitual criminals correspond to the lymphatic system. And the victims of the 'waves' form 'vast dense gray shoals like ocean herring'.[76]

Both the technological and the organic in Solzhenitsyn's organising imagery seem to propose structures and processes independent of human agency or control; and for Solzhenitsyn's idea of history, control is the crucial question. The role of the individual within history, the extent to which he can be held responsible or can change his situation is left unexplained. The imagery of the Great Machine perhaps presupposes the Great Mechanic who originally constructed the device, and indeed when Solzhenitsyn's technocratic ideology issues out into prescriptive injunctions its very substance is a belief in an individual or collective elite who should run society and its institutions. But the technical and structural images are not used in this way. Although one of the intentions of *The Gulag Archipelago* is to demonstrate a continuity between Lenin and Stalin, to prove the former an architect of later repression, the emphasis of these technological images of history is upon mechanical operations which take place over against the activities of individuals, including those people who apparently administer them. Yet the individual is, for Solzhenitsyn, the absolute subject of history: 'The Universe has as many different centers as there are living beings in it. Each of us is a center of the Universe.'[77] The individual is consequently expected to have moral responsibility and, in Solzhenitsyn's phrase, 'civil valor',[78] a concept upon which he puts much emphasis although it is ill-defined. He assigns to every Russian person some blame for having allowed the Stalinist crimes to take place. He chides the passivity of the arrestees (including himself) and, paradoxically, in view of the categorical condemnations of violence he has issued, Solzhenitsyn advocates—or at least speculates on the efficacy of—armed resistance:

> What would things have been like if every Security operative . . . had been uncertain whether he would return alive . . ? . . . We didn't love freedom enough . . . We spent ourselves in . . . 1917, and then we *hurried* to submit . . . We purely and simply *deserved* everything that happened afterward.[79]

This tendency to see historical processes in individual-moral terms, as questions of desire and deserving, is deeply embedded in Solzhenitsyn's historical understanding: for him it is in 'the history of *morals*' that 'everything else originates as well'.[80] This idealism permeates the ideology thoroughly and yet coexists uneasily with structural and organic forces simultaneously at work. The precise status of individual agency and accountability is ambiguous and this is exemplified by his attitude to Stalin. His general view is that Stalinism was criminal—as distinct from, say, Sholokhov's view that it was tragic—and Stalin, with a few individuals around him, was principally culpable, a criminal, and in some sense a personal initiator of the historical nexus that bears his name.[81] And yet Solzhenitsyn also says that he decided very early on that Stalin had set the Soviet Union on the wrong course but when he died there was no change of course. 'Events' seem to exist in an objective external sense and Stalin could only make a marginal 'imprint' on them, while 'in all the rest he followed the beaten path exactly as it had been signposted'.[82] Stalin is either an author of history *or* merely a functionary of a degenerative process already set in motion.

This image of a signposted path which the individual simply follows is significantly connected with the teleology characteristic of Solzhenitsyn's attempts to perceive Stalinist repression in the very first months and years of the revolution. Solzhenitsyn's account of *Bolshevik* repression is prejudiced and imaginative. He resorts, for example, to enumerating the categories of people who *could* have been arrested according to various quotations from Lenin which he tears from context. Working from the published speeches of Krylenko, chief state prosecutor from 1918 to 1931, he itemises (in another 'technological' rather than inherent structuring of his material) a number of trials which he uses in an attempt to illustrate the arbitrary and unjust nature of the early Soviet courts. Yet, almost in spite of himself, Solzhenitsyn tells us that under the Bolsheviks the accused were able to defend themselves freely, confessions were not extracted by torture, and sentences were lenient. Corrective labour was often arranged so that the convicted person lived at home and worked on some public project. The cases themselves also militate against Solzhenitsyn's argument. The 'Case of the Three Prosecutors'[83] recounts the prosecution of three corrupt *state* officials *by the state*; and in a further case to which Solzhenitsyn refers another official, Kosyrev, this time a member of the Control and Auditing Commission of the Cheka itself, was shot for his part in corrupt dealings.[84] Far from indicating gratuitous repression, these cases suggest that the workers' state was carefully regulating the activity of its officials. The clearest example of Solzhenitsyn's attempt to perceive *Stalinist* arbitrariness under the Bolsheviks is the trial he calls 'The Case of the Suicide of Engineer Oldenborger'.[85] As Mandel points out,[86] it is not until the reader is deep into Solzhenitsyn's account of the trial that it becomes clear that the state is prosecuting three *Communists* who had persecuted to the point of suicide an apolitical but efficient engineer in the Moscow water supply system who had been elected to his post by the workers. What emerges from this is Solzhenitsyn's readiness to distort the earlier period so that it resembles the absence of legality under Stalin in order to prove that Stalinism followed inevitably and without break from the initial Bolshevik regime! The argument is perfectly circular, presupposing its conclusions in order to prove them.

To return to the image of the signposted path and the ambiguity this reveals in Solzhenitsyn's attitude to individual agency, it can now be seen that this image reflects the historical prejudice in his account of the Bolsheviks. The following of a path implies those who went before and marked the route. Yet Solzhenitsyn does not tell us who those agents were. Like the machine of Stalinist repression, the initiator is not identified. The point is emphasised by a further image of ambiguous agency which Solzhenitsyn uses to describe the path from revolution to Stalinism: Solzhenitsyn imagines the process of history as the work of a painter, an over-all authorial agent, sketching in 1922 what he will paint fully later on.[87] But the painter is not present in history. He is not Lenin, nor even Stalin; and, crucially, the continuity of his work has to be perceived by 'us', a spectatorial audience, as if we through our perception (or 'divination') of history create rather than discover its immanent pattern. The idea of an individual author of history (who nevertheless remains unknown) and the necessity of an audience whose expectations modify the painter's work is a reflection of Solzhenitsyn's own authoritarian subjectivism.

The partiality behind the ambiguity of agency in Solzhenitsyn's view of history is revealed in his differing attitudes to Marxists on the one hand, and the Vlassovites on the other. When pleading mitigating circumstances for the latter who went over to the German armies and fought against the Soviet Union, he is prepared to cite absolute *social* determination of the actions of individuals: the 'Fatherland' was to blame for the treachery of the Vlassovites because it has to have had 'a social cause'.[88] And if this is not enough a resort can always be made to fatalism: most members of the Vlassovite military units found themselves in them by 'blind chance', it all depended, apparently on which recruiter went to which German camp for prisoners of war; had the Vlassovites been in different camps they might have become spies instead![89] But to be a Marxist, however, is an abdication from personal moral responsibility: 'Ideology—that is what gives evildoing its long-sought justification . . . That is the social theory which helps to make [the evildoer's] acts seem good.'[90] Apart from a misuse of the word 'ideology' what this passage reveals is marked divergence from Solzhenitsyn's indulgence towards members of a fascist army who are merely the objects of social forces or blind chance.

For all his attack on Marxism Solzhenitsyn does not reject the idea of laws of history altogether. He cites, for example, China's cultural revolution as an instance paralleling Stalin's 1937 of increased repression in the seventeenth year after the final victory of the revolution, which he regards as a fundamental law of historical development![91] But Solzhenitsyn offers no theoretical principle which would make such a law uniform and predictable—characteristics he demands of Soviet legality in order to ensure its objectivity. He invents a 'law' of history as a convenience to his argument, and this exposes the point that both his 'technocratic' and 'organicist' explanations of historical development, as well as the ambiguity of individual agency, are fundamentally and opportunistically ideological. Not only are they internally contradictory but they bear a mystified relationship to real history. Both the facts of Solzhenitsyn's 'investigation' and the conceptual structure within which they are displayed are mobilised not in the service of objective analysis but in pursuit of right-wing ideological objectives.

For all the concern in Solzhenitsyn's earlier peasant-orientated positions for 'common humanity', his elitism and authoritarianism in *The Gulag Archipelago* are explicit. He rejects genuine popular democracy not only in the present conjuncture of bureaucratic dictatorship but also as an historical possibility:

> How could *engineers* accept the *dictatorship of the workers* . . . their subordinates in industry, so little skilled or trained and comprehending neither the physical nor the economic laws of production . . . Why shouldn't the engineers have considered it more natural [sic] for the structure of society to be headed by those who could intelligently direct its activity?[92]

The class prejudice of a statement like this hardly requires comment. Solzhenitsyn subsequently suggests that technocracy is 'precisely where all social cybernetics is leading today'.[93] And 'social cybernetics', he implies, is a desirable alternative to democratic politics, for professional politicians are in any case no more than 'boils on the neck of society'. What is probably a just judgement on the parasitic bureaucracy that rules the Soviet Union today, when erected into a statement for all time only reinforces the overtness of Solzhenitsyn's advocacy of the replacement of the dictatorship of the bureaucracy with that of the technocrats.

As in other matters, the organic element of Solzhenitsyn's ideology parallels the technocratic, his religious positions evincing a moral authoritarianism. *The Gulag Archipelago* is not only an account of the apparatus of repression, it also charts Solzhenitsyn's own passage from Marxism to religious ideology. When arrested, his position was, in his own phrase, one of the advocacy of 'purified Leninism'[94]: he had decided that Stalin was responsible for the development of repression and Solzhenitsyn in prison defended Marxism. It is important to notice, however, that Solzhenitsyn's Marxism was itself ideological, a version of Stalinist dogmatism: he describes it as a world outlook 'incapable of admitting any new fact or evaluating any new opinion before a label has been found for it from the already available stock'.[95] This places the young Solzhenitsyn firmly in the centre of that alienated ideological Marxism which appears in the Soviet Union as a state religion.[96] And thus Solzhenitsyn was prepared for a retreat into mysticism before his personal confrontation with the state provoked it.

Solzhenitsyn's break with Marxism began shortly after his imprisonment; he describes a meeting with another prisoner Borya Gammerov at which they discussed a prayer of Roosevelt's that had been published in the Soviet press. Gammerov's conviction that it was possible for a political leader to 'sincerely believe in God' startled the then still 'Marxist' Solzhenitsyn, but nonetheless exerted a powerful influence over him: 'To hear such words from someone born in 1923? I could have replied to him very firmly, but prison had already undermined my certainty . . .'[97] 'Prison had already undermined my certainty'—he acknowledges that the experience of repression had itself initiated the retreat from Marxism. But there is a more positive side: as Mandel remarks, Solzhenitsyn, particularly where he deals with the show trials and the extraordinary confessions of the accused, generally confirms Trotsky's conclusions that the 'lack of a political perspective independent of Stalinism (that is the political capitulation of Stalin's unfortunate victims before the bureaucratic dictatorship) was the real basis of the confessions'.[98] The belief that even their own arrest and possible execution was in some mysterious way furthering the cause of socialism in the Soviet Union, sometimes underpinned by Stalin's absurd theory that the class struggle *intensifies* under socialism, led even party militants to cooperate fully in their own destruction.

Yet the alternative to capitulation that Solzhenitsyn offers is not a political one at all, but one of religious propagandising combined with an utterly passive inner resilience. He recounts an anecdote clearly of great importance to him about the prisoner Vera Korneyeva who, when left in an office with clerical employees of the MGB, began to deliver a sermon. Even though in freedom she had been 'no more' [sic] than a lathe operator, stable girl and 'housewife', she had a 'gift of eloquence' and sufficiently impressed her audience for them to silence the interruptions of Korneyeva's interrogator when he returned to the room so that she could finish her speech against the persecution of religious believers in silence. While the anecdote represents in however mediated a way a kind of active opposition carried out, in this case, at the very heart of the Organs, in the offices of the MGB itself, it is, for Solzhenitsyn, but the infrequent manifestation of what is essentially an inner state. When the same prisoner managed to prevail upon her interrogator to let her sign depositions implicating only herself, rather than ones which would incriminate others in her religious group, she experiences a 'feeling of spiritual victory', and for Solzhenitsyn it is this *feeling* which is central:

> Submissiveness to fate, the total abdication of your own will in the shaping of your life . . . all this freed the prisoner from any bondage . . . and even ennobled him.[99]

This passage enacts Solzhenitsyn's willingness to spiritualise the experience of repression. From an important description of the way in which the prisoner knows himself to be at the mercy of forces external to and stronger than himself, forces which are politically and sociologically knowable but may appear in mystified form as 'fate', it topples over into an endorsement of the psychological state of the prisoner; he is 'ennobled' by his total loss of freedom. For the authoritarian, the individual receives this aristocratic elevation at the precise moment when he loses all agency. In order to validate this seemingly (and actually) untenable belief that captivity—not willing service of the traditional Christian understanding—is in fact a form of exquisite freedom, Solzhenitsyn has necessarily to invoke the familiar idealist dichotomy between the corporeal and the spiritual:

> My name? I am the Interstellar Wanderer! They have tightly bound my body, but my soul is beyond their power.[100]

The prisoner, because his will has been taken from him and, according to Solzhenitsyn, has been freed by deprivation from material concerns, can enter 'the heavenly kingdom of the liberated spirit' with 'a newly dawning enlightenment'.[101] Not only does this mystificatory idealisation of repression contradict other descriptions Solzhenitsyn gives of prison behaviour in which he emphasises the ruthless competitive individualism which the prisoners must adopt if they are to survive, but it reaches beyond the level of individual psychology; he gives the 'liberated spirit' a clear national and political environment. He describes admiringly a White colonel, Konstantin Yesevich, who, in contrast to Solzhenitsyn's own 'spiritual confusion' (shortly after his arrest), had a 'clear and exact view of everything around him; as a result of this reasoned point of view on life, his body, too, exhibited a steady strength, resiliency, and activity'.[102] Solzhenitsyn confesses not to know whether this paragon was amongst those White Guards who 'hung every tenth worker and whipped the peasants'. At the national level the spiritualised experience of the prisoner whom Solzhenitsyn, in the context of tireless vituperation against the professional criminals he encountered in the camps, compares to 'Christ crucified between two thieves . . . numbered with the transgressors', becomes the *necessity* of defeat in war which engenders for the nation 'a spiritual upsurge' analogous to 'the deepening of the inner life' of the persecuted individual.[103]

The idealisation of repression reaches its zenith in Part IV of *The Gulag Archipelago* which is entitled 'The Soul and Barbed Wire'. In particular Chapter One articulates most clearly Solzhenitsyn's mystificatory belief in the beneficial changes of character that prisoners undergo. Founded on the remarkable assumption that 'It has been known for many centuries that prison causes the profound rebirth of a human being',[104] this chapter, which is called 'The Ascent', charts the supposed passage of the 'soul' from the turmoil of arrest to an impassive inner serenity. It is sometimes only after years in the camps, when the more complicated world of freedom has been left far behind, that the prisoner achieves that mildness and tolerance when 'Your eyes do not flash with gladness over good tidings nor do they darken with grief'.[105] Instead the prisoner, who is the 'crown of creation', provided that he resists the temptation to collaborate with the camp authorities at the expense of his comrades and thus passes that 'great fork in the camp road . . . that great divider of souls', attains an apprehension that 'the meaning of earthly existence lies . . . in the development of the soul'.[106] He is 'purified by suffering'. This is not, of course, without its political implications. Solzhenitsyn, who ends his chapter with an ecstatic '*Bless you, prison*, for having been in my life', carries away from this apotheosis the understanding that all revolutions are to be condemned because they only destroy the contemporary carriers of evil, and then immediately assume, in magnified form, the 'evil' they overthrew. The central struggle, becomes, in a final foregrounding of the individual subject and a last rejection of history, the struggle 'with the evil inside a human being'.

It is here, in Solzhenitsyn's preparedness to mystify and mythologise the experience of terrible repression, transforming it into a transcendency, 'that glimmering light . . . the soul of the lonely prisoner begins to emit, like the halo of a saint', a state in which 'even counting the passing minutes puts him intimately in touch with the Universe', that the full distance has been travelled from *One Day in the Life of Ivan Denisovich*. Where once the prisoner was depicted as an isolated victim of state terrorism, alienated by the atomisation of Soviet society, now he becomes an abstract Prisoner, detached from 'the hustle-bustle of everyday life . . . purged of every imperfection' whose 'head rises of itself towards the Eternal Heavens'.[107] The 'critical empiricism' of the earlier work is replaced by the explicit ideological intention of *The Gulag Archipelago*, and, where previously the structure of absolute valuations under which the 'fact' of *One Day in the Life of Ivan Denisovich* was subsumed was left undisruptively 'external' to the work itself, Solzhenitsyn now conscientiously articulates an ideology which is politically reactionary, socially and morally elitist, and in the end devoid of artistic interest. At the very moment when the, as it were, non-fictive status of the first book is acknowledged by the historiographical form of the later, *The Gulag Archipelago* reveals itself as the greater fiction. *Ivan Denisovich* enacted a less articulated but less oblique relationship to objective history.

Notes

1 INTRODUCTION

1   K. Simonov, 'About the past in the name of the future', *Izvestia* (Moscow, 18 November 1962), reprinted in L. Labedz, *Solzhenitsyn: A Documentary Record* (Harmondsworth: Penguin, 1972) p. 41.

2   P. Zhilin, 'How A. Solzhenitsyn sang of the Vlasovites' [sic] Betrayal', *Izvestia* (Moscow, 28 January 1974), reprinted in *The Last Circle* (Novosti Press Agency Publishing House, 1974) p. 102.

3   See Home, 'The lesson we could learn from this man out of chains . . .' *Sunday Express* (London, 5 January 1975).

4   See Labedz, op. cit., p. 15.

5   E. Harding, 'Opposition currents in the USSR', *International*, vol 2, no 1.

6   ibid.

7   See E. Mandel, 'Solzhenitsyn, Stalinism and the October Revolution', *New Left Review*, 86 (1974) pp. 51–61.

8   A. Solzhenitsyn, *Cancer Ward* (Harmondsworth: Penguin, 1971) p. 472.

9   There are considerable problems involved in dating Solzhenitsyn's writing, problems which are not primarily chronological but critical. The neatness of the segregation of the work into 'early' and 'late' that has been adopted here is to a certain extent confounded by the complexity of the process of ideological development itself. *The Gulag Archipelago* for example clearly belongs ideologically to the later period of Solzhenitsyn's writing although it is based on many years' research and the actual composition spanned the years 1958 to 1972 (if the author's latest amendments are included), and much of the work was completed by 1966 before the start of the later period. Similarly *August 1914* has a somewhat ambiguous chronological status: the text is dated 1969–70 but as early as 1937 Solzhenitsyn wrote a long essay on 'The Samsonov Disaster' which might now be regarded as a very early draft for the novel. Yet this does not overthrow the argument for the increasing 'ideologisation' of the writing but merely denies that this is a *rigidly* linear process. The critic is deprived of any easy sequentiality. The complexity of the relationship between Solzhenitsyn's personal views and the ideology of his fiction is a case in point here. The novels in the early period of his work could be seen as corresponding to the 'purified Leninism' that Solzhenitsyn espoused before his imprisonment. He abandoned this position as a personal viewpoint in 1946: it only disappears from his fiction in the mid-sixties.

10 See C. Moody, *Solzhenitsyn* (Edinburgh: Oliver and Boyd, 1973) p. 17.

11 'High Requirements', *Pravda* (Moscow, 11 April 1964), reprinted in

Labedz, op. cit., p. 76.

12 'Moscow writers on *Cancer Ward*', ibid., pp. 83–105.

13 ibid., p. 21; see also p. 156.

14 'Alexander Tvardovsky to Konstantin Fedin', ibid., p. 158.

15 A. Solzhenitsyn, *The First Circle*, trans. M. Guybon (London: Collins/ Fontana, 1970) p. 306.

16 ibid., p. 390.

17 ibid., p. 390.

18 ibid., pp. 357–8.

2 THE 'DEMOCRATIC' NOVELS

1 *The First Circle*, p. 51.

2 ibid., pp. 88–9.

3 ibid., p. 335.

4 *Cancer Ward*, pp. 40–1.

5 ibid., p. 31.

6 ibid., p. 148.

7 ibid., p. 570.

8 ibid., p. 570.

9 A. Solzhenitsyn, *One Day in the Life of Ivan Denisovich*, trans. R. Parker (Harmondsworth: Penguin, 1963) p. 143.

10 See C. Moody, *Solzhenitsyn* (Edinburgh: Oliver and Boyd, 1973) p. 62.

11 *One Day in the Life* . . ., p. 75, emphasis added.

12 'Address at the Nobel Festival by Dr Karl Ragnar Gierow' in L. Labedz *Solzhenitsyn: A Documentary Record* (Harmondsworth: Penguin, 1972) pp. 252–3.

13 *One Day in the Life* . . ., p. 139.

14 ibid., p. 40.

15 ibid., p. 32.

16 See H. Ticktin, 'Political Economy of the Soviet Intellectual', *Critique*, 2, pp. 5–21.

17 'Letter from Solzhenitsyn to three students', in Labedz, op. cit., p. 151.

18 G. Lukács, *Solzhenitsyn*, trans. W. D. Graf (London: Merlin, 1970) p. 13.

19 Quoted in Moody, op. cit., p. 48.

20 *One Day in the Life* . . ., p. 63.

21 A. Solzhenitsyn, *An Incident at Krechetovka Station* in *We Never Make Mistakes*, trans. P. W. Blackstock (London: Sphere, 1972) pp. 86–7.

22 Moody, op. cit., p. 105ff.

23 *The First Circle*, p. 134.

24 This interpretation of the function of the figure of Stalin may be reinforced by the example of the passages in *The First Circle* which deal with official literature. While they reflect Solzhenitsyn's personal preoccupation with the state of Soviet literature, in the novel they have a similar function to that of the Stalin figure. Suffering, through their often arbitrary insertion, from a similar incongruity with the rest of the text, they also serve to specify and generalise the novel's account of the enervating effects of Stalinist ideology, underpinned by coercion, in all aspects of social life. Like the Stalin figure, they are ultimately less important for

what they 'say' than for what they 'do' in the text.
25 'Letter from Solzhenitsyn to three students', in Labedz, op. cit., p. 151.
26 A. Solzhenitsyn, *For the Good of the Cause* (London: Sphere, 1971).
27 T. Deutscher, 'Soviet Fabians and Others', *New Left Review*, 62 (1970) pp. 45–54.

3 AFTER DEMOCRACY
1 In L. Labedz, *Solzhenitsyn: A Documentary Record* (Harmondsworth: Penguin, 1972) pp. 106–12.
2 See ibid., pp. 112–26.
3 A. Solzhenitsyn, *Nobel Prize Lecture*, trans. N. Bethell (London: Stenvalley, 1973).
4 There is a hint in the *Lecture* that the reason for this is that art is not entirely a *human* product: Solzhenitsyn compares the failure of the artist who attempts to people an imaginary world with his own creations with the comparative success of one who acknowledges himself 'as a young apprentice under God's heaven . . . this world was not created by him [the artist] and is not ruled by him . . . There is no doubt who built its foundations.' p. 9.
5 ibid., p. 9.
6 ibid., p. 11.
7 ibid., p. 13.
8 ibid., p. 21.
9 ibid., p. 21.
10 ibid., p. 27.
11 ibid., p. 29.
12 ibid., p. 31.
13 ibid., pp. 37–9.
14 ibid., p. 39.
15 ibid., p. 39.
16 ibid., p. 41.
17 ibid., p. 37.
18 Not only writers, but scientists also should attack the 'spirit of Munich' which has drained their energy and prevented a proper social commitment. The remark here (p. 43) that 'the shape of the modern world is entirely in the hands of scientists' points forward to the technocratic elitism of *The Gulag Archipelago*.
19 ibid., p. 47.
20 ibid., p. 51.
21 A. Solzhenitsyn, *Letter to Soviet Leaders*, trans. H. Sternberg (London: Index on Censorship, 1974).
22 ibid., p. 15.
23 ibid., p. 20.
24 ibid., p. 12.
25 ibid., p. 25.
26 ibid., pp. 20–1.
27 ibid., p. 22.
28 ibid., pp. 33–4.

29   ibid., p. 37.
30   ibid., p. 38.
31   See ibid., p. 55.
32   ibid., pp. 50–2 emphasis added.
33   ibid., p. 51.
34   ibid., p. 52.
35   ibid., p. 52.
36   ibid., p. 53.
37   ibid., p. 48.
38   See for example ibid., p. 47, where ideology is characterised as 'storm-cloud' and 'epidemic'; and p. 44, where atheism is said to be the centre of Marxism.
39   A. Solzhenitsyn, *August 1914*, trans. M. Glenny (Harmondsworth: Penguin, 1974). Chapter 22, omitted from this edition at the author's request, is now to be found in *Lenin in Zurich*, trans. H. T. Willetts (London: Bodley Head, 1976).
40   *August 1914*, p. 126.
41   ibid., p. 122.
42   ibid., p. 109.
43   ibid., pp. 236–81.
44   ibid., p. 405.
45   ibid., p. 258.
46   Significantly, the character Obodovsky is based closely on a real engineer of the twenties, Pyotr Akimovich Palchinsky, who was eventually arrested and shot without trial in 1929. See *The Gulag Archipelago*, Vol 2, pp. 298–300.
47   *August 1914*, p. 591.
48   Compare *August 1914*, pp. 596–7 with *Letter to Soviet Leaders*, p. 27ff.
49   *August 1914*, pp. 599–608.
50   ibid., p. 423.
51   ibid., p. 431.
52   ibid., p. 429.
53   ibid., p. 507.
54   *The Gulag Archipelago* (Parts I and II) Vol 1, trans. T. P. Whitney (London: Collins/Fontana, 1974) and *The Gulag Archipelago* (Parts III and IV) Vol 2 (1976). There are altogether seven parts in three volumes of which the third has yet to appear in translation. GULAG is an acronym for Chief Administration of Corrective Labour Camps.
55   R. Medvedev, 'On Gulag Archipelago', trans. T. Deutscher, *New Left Review*, 85 (1974).
56   E. Mandel, 'Solzhenitsyn, Stalinism and the October Revolution', *New Left Review*, 86 (1974).
57   M. McAuley, 'Political change since Stalin', *Critique*, 2, pp. 23–36.
58   Quoted in *The Gulag Archipelago* 1, p. 48.
59   H. Ticktin, 'Political Economy of the Soviet Intellectual', *Critique*, 2, pp. 5–21, to which much of the following is indebted.
60   L. Trotsky, *Literature and Revolution*, trans. R. Strunsky (University of Michigan, 1971), p. 222.

106 *Solzhenitsyn: Politics and Form*

61 See *The Gulag Archipelago* 1, p. 269.
62 ibid., p. 161.
63 ibid., p. 197.
64 ibid., p. 26.
65 ibid., pp. 185–6.
66 ibid., p. 26, emphasis added.
67 ibid., p. 302, emphasis added.
68 See ibid., pp. 8–11.
69 See e.g. ibid., pp. 582–3.
70 In order these references are to ibid., title Part 1 ch. 2; p. 90; p. 478; title Part 1 ch. 7; p. 291.
71 ibid., p. 144.
72 ibid., p. 71.
73 ibid., p. 94.
74 ibid., p. 25.
75 ibid., pp. 155–6.
76 In order these references are to ibid., pp. 75; 335; 464; 369; 149; 237.
77 ibid., p. 3.
78 ibid., p. 462.
79 ibid., p. 13, n. 5.
80 ibid., p. 435.
81 Medvedev points out (op. cit.) that while Solzhenitsyn speaks of 'Stalinists' he has no concept called 'Stalinism'. Most of his references to Stalin himself are dropped out of the main text into footnotes: this obliqueness points the ambiguity.
82 *The Gulag Archipelago* 1, p. 613, n. 4.
83 ibid., p. 311.
84 ibid., p. 314.
85 ibid., p. 336.
86 Mandel, op. cit.
87 *The Gulag Archipelago* 1, p. 364.
88 ibid., p. 262.
89 ibid., p. 261.
90 ibid., p. 174.
91 ibid., p. 68; p. 35.
92 ibid., p. 390.
93 ibid., p. 391.
94 ibid., p. 135.
95 ibid., p. 613.
96 Cf. Ticktin, op. cit. This also reinforces the point Mandel makes about Solzhenitsyn's technocratic positions: while his ideology is anti-Stalinist, it remains within the Stalinist problematic.
97 *The Gulag Archipelago* 1, p. 612.
98 Mandel, op. cit.
99 *The Gulag Archipelago* 1, p. 56.
100 ibid., p. 595.
101 ibid., p. 546.
102 ibid., p. 267.

103 ibid., p. 272.
104 *The Gulag Archipelago* 2, p. 586.
105 ibid., p. 593.
106 ibid., p. 595.
107 *The Gulag Archipelago* 1, p. 483.

Index

Index

111